The God of Freedom and Life
A Commentary on the Book of Exodus

Stephen J. Binz

A Liturgical Press Book

THE LITURGICAL PRESS
Collegeville, Minnesota

6   7   8

Library of Congress Cataloging-in-Publication Data

Binz, Stephen J., 1955-
    The God of freedom and life : a commentary on the book of Exodus / Stephen J. Binz.
    p.   cm.
    ISBN: 0-8146-2260-7
    1. Bible. O.T. Exodus—Commentaries. I. Title.
BS1245.3.B56   1993   93-2104
222'.12077—dc20   CIP

Contents

Abbreviations

Gen—Genesis
Exod—Exodus
Lev—Leviticus
Num—Numbers
Deut—Deuteronomy
Josh—Joshua
Judg—Judges
Ruth—Ruth
1 Sam—1 Samuel
2 Sam—2 Samuel
1 Kgs—1 Kings
2 Kgs—2 Kings
1 Chr—1 Chronicles
2 Chr—2 Chronicles
Ezra—Ezra
Neh—Nehemiah
Tob—Tobit
Jdt—Judith
Esth—Esther
1 Macc—1 Maccabees
2 Macc—2 Maccabees
Job—Job
Ps(s)—Psalms(s)
Prov—Proverbs

Eccl—Ecclesiastes
Song—Song of Songs
Wis—Wisdom
Sir—Sirach
Isa—Isaiah
Jer—Jeremiah
Lam—Lamentations
Bar—Baruch
Ezek—Ezekiel
Dan—Daniel
Hos—Hosea
Joel—Joel
Amos—Amos
Obad—Obadiah
Jonah—Jonah
Mic—Micah
Nah—Nahum
Hab—Habakkuk
Zeph—Zephaniah
Hag—Haggai
Zech—Zechariah
Mal—Malachi
Matt—Matthew
Mark—Mark
Luke—Luke

John—John
Acts—Acts
Rom—Romans
1 Cor—1 Corinthians
2 Cor—2 Corinthians
Gal—Galatians
Eph—Ephesians
Phil—Philippians
Col—Colossians
1 Thess—1 Thessalonians
2 Thess—2 Thessalonians
1 Tim—1 Timothy
2 Tim—2 Timothy
Titus—Titus
Phlm—Philemon
Heb—Hebrews
Jas—James
1 Pet—1 Peter
2 Pet—2 Peter
1 John—1 John
2 John—2 John
3 John—3 John
Jude—Jude
Rev—Revelation

Preface

In my *The Passion and Resurrection Narratives of Jesus: A Commentary* (The Liturgical Press, 1989), I examined the "exodus" of Jesus, the core of the Christian Scriptures. In this work I explore the foundation of the Jewish faith, the journey of Exodus. I have tried to show that the very heart of our Judaic heritage is the quest for freedom and life. Genuine freedom and fullness of life was the divinely inspired purpose of both Moses and Jesus and it is the goal of all who follow in their footsteps. I hope the explanations and insights contained here will enrich the journey in faith of all who read it in company with the text of Exodus.

During the time of my biblical studies in Jerusalem, I traveled the route of the Exodus—from the pyramids and ruins of Egypt, through days of desert travel and mountain climbing in the Sinai, to the ancient and holy places of the land of Israel. People have always gone from the cities to the desert and to the mountains for an environment in which deeper self-discovery can occur. My journey from the city, through the desert and to the mountains, and back into the city is a symbol for the inner journey of my life as well. Through my own experiences, both in sharing ministry and vibrant life with others and in the quiet solitude of prayer and study, I have encountered God in fuller and richer ways.

I am grateful for my companions along the journey, especially my parents and family. I am grateful for Sr. Deborah Troillett and the community of Mount St. Mary Academy in Little Rock with whom I ministered for the past nine years, and for Sr. Yvonne Lerner and St. Mary Parish in Arkadelphia and St. John Parish in Malvern. I am appreciative of the staff of Little Rock Scripture Study with whom I work—Lilly Hess, Judy Hoelzeman, Nancy Lee Walters, and especially Cackie Upchurch who offered me invaluable advice during the writing

5

of this book. I am particularly grateful for the constant support and inspiration given to me by my brother Mike to whom I dedicate this work.

STEPHEN J. BINZ

Introduction

Significance of the Exodus

The Exodus event is ancient, yet always new. It is the foundational event in which Israel came to know Yahweh and to know themselves as a people. It is the experience from which we continue to know who God is and what it means to be God's people. The passage from bondage to freedom, from death to life, is the story of all God's people.

The revelation of God as the personal and mysterious divine presence acting in history to bring people to freedom and life is the very heart of Jewish and Christian faith. The Exodus was the crucial event. In that generation of forty years, Israel came to know Yahweh as the God of freedom and life. Indeed, the Exodus narratives are a proclamation of Israel's faith, for Israel's creed was the recital of God's saving deeds in history.

Israel's liberation from bondage and its establishment as a people was the decisive and definitive event of God's self-disclosure. Though God continued to be revealed in subsequent history, further understandings and actions of God were always seen in light of this primary event of revelation. From that time on, Israel would see everything in its national history from the perspective of that foundational event. The prophets continually called Israel back to faith in Yahweh "who brought you up out of the land of Egypt." The Exodus became the paradigm for describing God's activity in human history.

The recital of the Exodus narratives is always a call to new hope. Because God had heard Israel's cries and acted in the past, Israel could be certain that God would continue to remember the past and act in the present. God, who had rescued Israel from bondage and death, would continue to rescue and save. In Israel's ever-new experiences of delivery, Israel would come to know God more fully and in new ways.

At the time in which the Exodus narratives were put in their present form, the people of Israel were experiencing a "new exodus," a new experience of liberation from the captivity of Babylon and an opportunity to begin their life again. In every age, Israel knew that its future would take shape according to the same patterns with which their past had been formed.

For Israel the Exodus was never just a memory of the past; it was a living reality for every generation. By retelling the story and especially through celebrating the covenant in Israel's liturgy, the events of the past became present. When the people of Israel went up to the Temple to celebrate the covenant renewal, they were not just recalling Mount Sinai, but they were standing with Moses and their ancestors as that event became alive for them. Reciting the narrative in ritual ceremony was not just a telling about the past, it was also a description of the present moment. The saving presence of God, the God of freedom and life, was reestablished for every generation. Israel remains always the people of the Exodus.

This foundational revelation underlies every other aspect of the Hebrew and Christian Scriptures. The whole complex of affirmations about God found in the law, the prophets, the psalms, and the Gospels is rooted in the Exodus event. God is not abstract, static, and impartial; the God revealed in Exodus liberates, enlivens, redeems, calls, negotiates, forgives, challenges, and journeys. God is revealed in the real, human events of history.

Formation of the Exodus Narrative

The Book of Exodus was not intended as an eye-witness account of events as they happened. It is rather a testament of the faith of generations expressing the meaning of the historical events experienced by their ancestors. While the Book of Exodus is rooted in historical events, it was expressed by later generations who had remembered and celebrated those events for hundreds of years. The story was told and retold in such a way that the experience of past generations and the faith of contemporary generations merged with one another.

Though the historical event of Exodus occurred around 1250 B.C., the narrative was not put in its final form until the fifth or sixth century B.C. The rich and varied history of Israel lay between. The nucleus of Israel's tradition, originating with Moses, was continually combined with new experiences and new understandings of God. The narrative of Israel's Passover is influenced not only by the first Passover, but by Israel's long history of deliverance from distress. The narrative depicting the entire law of Israel as having been revealed to Moses on Mount Sinai, is the result of seven hundred years of Israel's discernment of God's will in its legal tradition. The narrative of Israel's construction of the sanctuary is told from the perspective of generations of liturgical worship in Israel. Moses transmitted to Israel the formative experience and the insights of faith from which the national identity and accompanying institutions evolved. Moses was the framer of the founding tradition, but God continued to reveal the divine nature and will to Israel through the ages.

The Book of Exodus is a rich tapestry of different traditions from various periods of Israel's life. Storytellers, poets, lawyers, and temple priests all contribute to its final form. Changes in literary styles, repetitions, insertions, and occasional inconsistencies in the text give us clues to the complex literary history of the work. The final redaction of the Book of Exodus contains at least three different versions of salvation history that have been woven together. These independent versions, written in different periods of Israel's history, are the principal literary sources of Exodus. A few words about each of these will be helpful.

The earliest source is the Yahwist tradition, written in Judea around the time of King Solomon (c. 950 B.C.). Scholars have named this the Yahwist tradition because of its consistent reference to God by the proper name *Yahweh*. This source is characterized by its colorful and popular language, often portraying God in terms which stress the divine closeness with humanity. It forms the basic narrative of Exodus.

Another source is the Elohist tradition, written in the prophetic circles of the northern kingdom in the eighth century B.C. It is characterized by its use of the noun for God, *Elohim*, rather than the personal name. It describes God as more distant from humanity, using mediators and messengers to convey the divine presence. It expresses a more critical attitude toward Israel, and emphasizes the breaking of the covenant.

The latest source is the Priestly tradition, edited in the priestly circles of the Jerusalem Temple at the time of the Exile in the sixth century B.C. It is the easiest to recognize within the fabric of the book. Emphasizing the majestic transcendence of God, its concern is with the liturgical and legal aspects of Israel's life. It told the story of the Exodus from the context of the exile, and is thus concerned with those parts of the narrative which formed the foundation of Israel's life of worship. It was the priestly editors who joined their own tradition with the two older narratives, the Yahwist and the Elohist.

The seams and discrepancies in the work are often an attempt by the final editors to preserve elements of differing traditions. Often the same story seems to be told in different ways, details seem to be contradictory, and there are disjointed elements throughout. Rather than trying to harmonize inconsistencies in the text, the editors sought to be faithful to the memories of the traditions they had received. No one tradition could claim an exclusive right to tell the whole story.

Yet, the final redaction is a masterful work of literature. Attention to its seams and inconsistencies must not obscure the singleness and continuity of the narrative. The present form of the canonical text is a deliberate arrangement of material intended to form Israel's normative understanding of God and of its relationship to God. The many traditions contained in Exodus, dating from the time of Moses all the way down to the Exile, express Israel's timeless faith in the God who was, who is, and who always will be.

Exodus and the Human Journey

Israel's encounter with the God of freedom and life has provided a hopeful context in which countless other communities and peoples have understood their own experiences. African-American people have expressed their struggles from the period of slavery to the civil rights movement with the language of Exodus. People imbued with a new spirit of Moses have called on new Pharaohs to "let my people go." The Jewish people of our century have expressed their persecutions and hopes, from the Holocaust to the declaration of a national homeland in Israel, within the context of faith provided by Exodus. The marginalized people of Latin America have reread Exodus in light of their own experiences of bondage and deliverance and have developed a theology and spirituality to express their new self-understanding. The paradigmatic narrative of liberation continually inflames the hopes and passions of oppressed people. New prophets, in the spirit of Moses, arise in every age to challenge people and societies to the demanding task of working for genuine human liberation from the bondage of sin, slavery, and death.

When we hear the words of the Exodus text within the depths of our own lives, we discover God's alternative vision of freedom and life and allow it to offer direction for our own journey. Israel's experience becomes our story and reveals to us the human drive and destiny to be free and fully alive. Readers of the Exodus text are invited to join Israel in the hunger for freedom, to stand with Moses at the burning bush and on the mountaintop, to experience the awesome and fascinating attractiveness of the divine presence.

The God of Exodus continues to intervene, rescuing us in desperate times and directing us to new understandings and new goals. We find within our lives new Pharaohs and new Egypts, people and situations that enslave and destroy life. We discover new Moses's, new deserts, new Sinais, and new promised lands. We locate people and experiences that reveal God to us, dangerous places of divine encounter, situations that liberate us and renew our lives. Like Israel, we fear the unknown, yet following God's initiative we leave what is secure and strike out on the journey. The experience of Exodus enables us to trust, to know that God who has been faithful in the past will be with us along the journey and will lead us to the fullness of life.

1:1-7 Jacob's Descendants in Egypt

¹These are the names of the sons of Israel who, accompanied by their households, migrated with Jacob into Egypt: ²Reuben, Simeon, Levi and Judah; ³Issachar, Zebulun and Benjamin; ⁴Dan and Naphtali; Gad and Asher. ⁵The total number of the direct descendants of Jacob was seventy. Joseph was already in Egypt.

⁶Now Joseph and all his brothers and that whole generation died. ⁷But the Israelites were fruitful and prolific. They became so numerous and strong that the land was filled with them.

The opening verses link the Exodus story with the ancestral narratives of Genesis. These traditions revealed a God who brought forth and fostered life for Abraham and his descendants. The narratives of Genesis 37–50 describe how Joseph, who had been sold into slavery by his jealous brothers, rose to prominence in Egypt. Later when the life of his family was threatened by a famine in Canaan, Joseph provided for his father Jacob and his brothers when they came seeking food in Egypt. Though he had been enslaved and his life threatened by his brothers, Joseph saved their lives and allowed them to remain in Egypt.

Verse six indicates the passage to a new era. The twelve sons of Jacob (Israel) had died. Through the passage of several generations, that family had become the people of Israel. Five Hebrew verbs in verse seven describe an extraordinary increase in the number of God's people. God's intentions for humanity at creation, to be fruitful and multiply, and God's promises to Abraham, to make his descendants a great nation, were being fulfilled. The focus of Exodus is the formation of this multitude into the people of God.

1:8-14 The Oppression

⁸Then a new king, who knew nothing of Joseph, came to power in Egypt. ⁹He said to his subjects, "Look how numerous and power-

ful the Israelite people are growing, more so than we ourselves! ¹⁰Come, let us deal shrewdly with them to stop their increase; otherwise, in time of war they too may join our enemies to fight against us, and so leave our country."

¹¹Accordingly, taskmasters were set over the Israelites to oppress them with forced labor. Thus they had to build for Pharaoh the supply cities of Pithom and Raamses. ¹²Yet the more they were oppressed, the more they multiplied and spread. The Egyptians, then, dreaded the Israelites ¹³and reduced them to cruel slavery, ¹⁴making life bitter for them with hard work in mortar and brick and all kinds of field work—the whole cruel fate of slaves.

"Pharaoh" was the title for the kings of Egypt. The new Pharaoh, who had no appreciation of the accomplishments of Joseph, caused the situation to change for the Israelites. The Pharaoh of this oppression was probably Seti I, who was succeeded by Ramses II, the Pharaoh of the Exodus. Excavations indicate that this dynasty undertook a vast building project in the delta region of the Nile in which they engaged the slave labor of foreigners. Since the area was on the eastern frontier where enemies often invaded Egypt, the king feared that the Israelites would ally themselves with Egypt's enemies in case of an invasion.

The Pharaoh is purposely left unnamed. As the narrative takes on epic proportions, he becomes a symbol for the forces of slavery and death which take on the God of freedom and life. Israel's blessing of abundant life led to fear in the king of Egypt. His fears became structured into the oppressive system of slavery and soon led to the destruction of life. Though slavery had become an accepted and unchangeable institution for Egypt, it was totally contrary to Israel's understanding of God's purpose for them. Indeed, the more they were oppressed, the more abundant they grew.

Verses 13-14 stress the intensity of Israel's experience of oppression. The writer uses a series of Hebrew words which are all forms of the Hebrew root "serve." The service of the Pharaoh implies bondage and death. Yet, the same word is later used for the service and worship of God (3:12). Only in the service of God can Israel discover its purpose and experience genuine freedom.

1:15-22 Command to the Midwives

¹⁵The king of Egypt told the Hebrew midwives, one of whom was called Shiphrah and the other Puah, ¹⁶"When you act as midwives

for the Hebrew women and see them giving birth, if it is a boy, kill him; but if it is a girl, she may live." [17]The midwives, however, feared God; they did not do as the king of Egypt had ordered them, but let the boys live. [18]So the king summoned the midwives and asked them, "Why have you acted thus, allowing the boys to live?" [19]The midwives answered Pharaoh, "The Hebrew women are not like the Egyptian women. They are robust and give birth before the midwife arrives." [20]Therefore God dealt well with the midwives. The people, too, increased and grew strong. [21]And because the midwives feared God, he built up families for them. [22]Pharaoh then commanded all his subjects, "Throw into the river every boy that is born to the Hebrews, but you may let all the girls live."

Having failed to utterly suppress the Israelites with harsh servitude, the king of Egypt ordered the murder of the male children of the Hebrews. Ironically he chose professional life-bearers, the midwives, to be his instruments of death. Because the Hebrew midwives respected ("feared") God, they knew that the preservation of life took precedence over the murderous decrees of the king, even at the risk of their own lives.

Recording the names of the two women invites a familiarity with them in contrast to the nameless oppressor. Women, often powerless in ancient societies, are given a crucial role in promoting the life of Israel. Indeed, all the Israelite women are said to be robust and lively, serving the cause of life. Two powerless women silence the power of Egypt. God worked through the courage and commitment of these two women to enable Israel to continue to flourish. God rewarded their reverence for the offspring of others by giving them children of their own.

Having failed again, Pharaoh initiates his third policy of oppression, the command to drown in the Nile all the boys born to the Hebrews. Ironically, each form of oppression portends the eventual triumph of Israel. The midwives, in saving the sons from death, foreshadow the saving activity of God in the Passover. The drowning of the boys in the Nile anticipates the way Pharaoh and his armies will meet their death. The oppressive actions, finally, prepare the way for the story of Moses' birth.

2:1-10 Birth and Adoption of Moses

[1]Now a certain man of the house of Levi married a Levite woman, [2]who conceived and bore a son. Seeing that he was a goodly child,

she hid him for three months. ³When she could hide him no longer, she took a papyrus basket, daubed it with bitumen and pitch, and putting the child in it, placed it among the reeds on the river bank. ⁴His sister stationed herself at a distance to find out what would happen to him.

⁵Pharaoh's daughter came down to the river to bathe, while her maids walked along the river bank. Noticing the basket among the reeds, she sent her handmaid to fetch it. ⁶On opening it, she looked, and lo, there was a baby boy, crying! She was moved with pity for him and said, "It is one of the Hebrews' children." ⁷Then his sister asked Pharaoh's daughter, "Shall I go and call one of the Hebrew women to nurse the child for you?" ⁸"Yes, do so," she answered. So the maiden went and called the child's own mother. ⁹Pharaoh's daughter said to her, "Take this child and nurse it for me, and I will repay you." The woman therefore took the child and nursed it. ¹⁰When the child grew, she brought him to Pharaoh's daughter, who adopted him as her son and called him Moses; for she said, "I drew him out of the water."

Pharaoh's decree of death is again thwarted by women. His command to "let all the girls live" comes back at him as the combined efforts of three women avert his plan for violence and death. Moses' mother saves him by literally following the orders of Pharaoh to put her child in the river. Later she emerges to be the nurse of her own son, and is even paid for her service from the royal treasury. The daughter of Pharaoh, the child of the oppressor, sees the child of the oppressed and is moved with pity. His own daughter saves the very person who would destroy the power of Pharaoh and lead his people to freedom. Moses' sister serves as the intermediary and brings together his biological and adoptive mother in an ironic conspiracy that results in the life of Israel's deliverer.

As the story of Moses' birth took shape within Hebrew tradition, it is probable that some motifs, such as dramatic rescue and royal education, were influenced by the heroic folklore of the Near East. Yet, the author used themes from these sources to dramatically link Moses with the oppression of his people and to foreshadow his future role. From the moment of his birth, he suffered the oppression and the ban of death from which he would deliver his people. The one who would lead Israel from the bondage of Pharaoh grew up and was educated in Pharaoh's own palace. What the daughter of Pharaoh did for Moses anticipates what God will do for Israel. She came down, saw the child and heard its cry, was moved with pity, rescued it from the waters, and provided for its care.

Pharaoh's means of destruction, the waters of the Nile, became the means for saving Moses. A helpless baby in a fragile basket became the means of God's manifestation of power. The instrument of Moses' rescue, the basket or "ark," is the same Hebrew word used for the ark of Noah in Genesis. The threatening waters of destruction again become the instrument of freedom and life.

The name "Moses" is actually of Egyptian origin meaning "born of" or "son of." In Egyptian names the root is often coupled with the name of a deity; i.e., Tutmoses and Ramses. Yet, the Hebrews often discovered popular etymologies for foreign names. The Hebrew *Mosheh* is an active participle meaning "one who draws out." His rescue from the waters is a foreshadowing of his future role. Before he can draw out his people, he must himself be drawn out.

2:11-22 Moses' Flight to Midian

[11]On one occasion, after Moses had grown up, when he visited his kinsmen and witnessed their forced labor, he saw an Egyptian striking a Hebrew, one of his own kinsmen. [12]Looking about and seeing no one, he slew the Egyptian and hid him in the sand. [13]The next day he went out again, and now two Hebrews were fighting! So he asked the culprit, "Why are you striking your fellow Hebrew?" [14]But he replied, "Who has appointed you ruler and judge over us? Are you thinking of killing me as you killed the Egyptian?" Then Moses became afraid and thought, "The affair must certainly be known."

[15]Pharaoh, too, heard of the affair and sought to put him to death. But Moses fled from him and stayed in the land of Midian. As he was seated there by a well, [16]seven daughters of a priest of Midian came to draw water and fill the troughs to water their father's flock. [17]But some shepherds came and drove them away. Then Moses got up and defended them and watered their flock. [18]When they returned to their father Reuel, he said to them, "How is it you have returned so soon today?" [19]They answered, "An Egyptian saved us from the interference of the shepherds. He even drew water for us and watered the flock!" [20]"Where is the man?" he asked his daughters. "Why did you leave him there? Invite him to have something to eat." [21]Moses agreed to live with him, and the man gave him his daughter Zipporah in marriage. [22]She bore

him a son, whom he named Gershom; for he said, "I am a stranger in a foreign land."

The Hebrew Scripture is silent on the period of Moses' youth and education. Typical of biblical literature, many details of his life have been omitted, with the text focused on those elements related to the liberation of God's people. Moses is seen here in three short episodes from his adult life which indicate his character. His central concern in each episode is justice for the victims, though he pursues that justice in an impetuous and violent way.

Moses responds to the injustice of three different peoples against three different types of victims. First, an Egyptian oppressor is beating a Hebrew slave; second, a Hebrew is maltreating a fellow Hebrew; and third, nomadic men are depriving women of what is theirs by right. In each scene Moses shows the courage to risk his own life for others and an intolerance for the abuse of the weak by those with power. Each incident also prepares for what is to follow in the narrative by providing a transition and a foreshadowing.

The first episode shows that although Moses was brought up in the palace of Egypt, he allied himself with the oppressed Hebrews. Seeing the injustice done to his people, Moses responds with action by striking the Egyptian. His conflict with the Egyptian and his fleeing from the land into the wilderness anticipates what his people will soon experience.

The second scene demonstrates that issues of justice must be addressed within the Israelite community as well. Moses' authority to intervene and confront his own people is challenged. His credentials as ruler and judge are questioned. This will be the continuing struggle of Moses with his people as they often reject his authority and refuse to listen to him during their experience in the desert.

The third episode takes place as Moses has fled out of Egypt and into the wilderness. His flight foreshadows the escape of Israel from Egypt into the desert. There, as a sojourner in the desert, Moses discovers his own alien identity as an Israelite, just as the people will come to know themselves in this same wilderness.

When the daughters of the priest of Midian were driven away by the shepherds, Moses delivered them and provided water for their flocks. There in a foreign land, his concern for the abused creates an alliance with the people of Midian which was expressed in their hospitality and the eventual marriage of Moses. His wife Zipporah (meaning "bird") gave birth to their son Gershom, whose name expresses Moses' experience as a stranger without a true home. His state as an alien both in Egypt and in Midian anticipates his call to lead his people to their promised land.

Moses' sympathy for the downtrodden and his desire to liberate those who are treated unjustly anticipates the saving will of God demonstrated throughout the Exodus. From the beginning Moses is presented as a man who transcends the narrow bounds of his own people. He was brought up as an Egyptian, he spent much of his adult life sojourning among the Midianite people, and he even married outside the community of Israel. The call to freedom and life creates broad alliances and anticipates the fulfillment of God's promise (Gen 12:3) to make Israel a blessing to all the communities of the earth.

2:23–3:3 The Burning Bush

> [23]A long time passed, during which the king of Egypt died. Still the Israelites groaned and cried out because of their slavery. As their cry for release went up to God, [24]he heard their groaning and was mindful of his covenant with Abraham, Isaac and Jacob. [25]He saw the Israelites and knew. . . .
>
> 3 [1]Meanwhile Moses was tending the flock of his father-in-law Jethro, the priest of Midian. Leading the flock across the desert, he came to Horeb, the mountain of God. [2]There an angel of the LORD appeared to him in fire flaming out of a bush. As he looked on, he was surprised to see that the bush, though on fire, was not consumed. [3]So Moses decided, "I must go over to look at this remarkable sight, and see why the bush is not burned."

A new era begins with the death of the Pharaoh and the beginning of God's direct action on behalf of the deliverance of the people in bondage. The dead oppressor, Seti I, was succeeded by the Pharaoh of the Exodus, Ramses II. As often happened in the Near East, the death of an unpopular ruler became the signal for rebellion by subject people. It was the lament of the people, their groaning and crying out, that was the turning point. When the people became aware of the injustice done to them and cried out against it, God responded and began their liberation.

Up to this point in the narrative God had remained hidden. Here the Hebrew text repetitively insists that God is the subject of four verbs: "God heard . . . God remembered . . . God saw . . . God knew."

God listened and responded to the outcry of the people. God's covenant made with Abraham, Isaac, and Jacob became activated again through God's remembering. God saw the suffering and oppression of the people of Israel and looked upon them with pity. Then God knew it was time for action on behalf of the people in bondage.

The beginning of God's response was the encounter with Moses. It is the primal elements of the created world—the desert, the mountain, the fire—that become the means of divine self-revelation. The desert, with its mysterious silence and dryness, enables Moses to experience God's presence and would become the place for Israel's bonding to God. The mountain, mysteriously reaching into the clouds, became an instrument of encounter with God and the place where all Israel would experience the call of God. Though this mountain has traditionally been associated with Jebel Musa in the southern part of the Sinai peninsula, the text is not concerned with such geographical remembrances. The unconsuming fire draws Moses to the site of God's manifestation. This unformed, elusive medium becomes a frequent expression of divine presence and purpose.

The combination of traditions represented by the final text of Exodus frequently uses different names for the same reality. Moses' father-in-law, here named "Jethro," had previously been referred to by his clan name "Reuel." The mountain of God is here called "Horeb" by the Elohist tradition, and "Sinai" by the Yahwist and Priestly traditions.

The initiative for this encounter is with God. Moses, concerned only with his daily activity of shepherding, is suddenly and unexpectedly met by God. The Hebrew imagination would not have asked whether the burning bush was a natural or miraculous phenomenon. They simply knew that God was the cause of all the wonders of the created world and such an unusual sight would have drawn Moses toward the presence of this mystery. The word translated "angel" is not a personal messenger, but any visible form under which God is manifested. With the initiative of God who acts in total freedom, any natural wonder can become a true theophany or sacrament of the divine presence.

Moses' shepherding the flock across the desert foreshadows his leading the people of Israel through the wilderness. His encounter with God at the mountain prepares for the experience of God by all the people at that same mountain. The word for the bush (*seneh*) is a verbal link to Sinai. Moses' experience of God in the burning *seneh* anticipates the manifestation of God at the fiery Sinai.

19

3:4-12 The Call of Moses

⁴When the Lord saw him coming over to look at it more closely, God called out to him from the bush, "Moses! Moses!" He answered, "Here I am." ⁵God said, "Come no nearer! Remove the sandals from your feet, for the place where you stand is holy ground. ⁶I am the God of your father," he continued, "the God of Abraham, the God of Isaac, the God of Jacob." Moses hid his face, for he was afraid to look at God. ⁷But the Lord said, "I have witnessed the affliction of my people in Egypt and have heard their cry of complaint against their slave drivers, so I know well what they are suffering. ⁸Therefore I have come down to rescue them from the hands of the Egyptians and lead them out of that land into a good and spacious land, a land flowing with milk and honey, the country of the Canaanites, Hittites, Amorites, Perizzites, Hivites and Jebusites. ⁹So indeed the cry of the Israelites has reached me, and I have truly noted that the Egyptians are oppressing them. ¹⁰Come, now! I will send you to Pharaoh to lead my people, the Israelites, out of Egypt."

¹¹But Moses said to God, "Who am I that I should go to Pharaoh and lead the Israelites out of Egypt?" ¹²He answered, "I will be with you; and this shall be your proof that it is I who have sent you: when you bring my people out of Egypt, you will worship God on this very mountain."

Moses is called to be God's spokesperson, a messenger of the word of God, despite opposition and personal shortcomings. The mission of Moses is the prototype of the many other calls that will follow in the history of salvation. Of all the vocation narratives in the Bible, this is the longest and most memorable. The three elements of Moses' call presented here become the pattern of many other call narratives; i.e., Gideon, Saul, Isaiah, Jeremiah. First, God chooses and commissions an unlikely individual for a difficult task; second, the one called objects, usually with good reason, that he is unworthy or incapable of fulfilling the mission; and third, God reassures the chosen one with the promise of divine presence and often a tangible sign.

The moment of encounter came as God called to Moses by name. Moses indicates his readiness and openness to God's word by his response: "Here I am." For Moses the experience of the Holy was one of fascinating attraction and trembling fear. The place became holy because it was sanctified or set apart for God's special purpose. Moses was asked to show respect in the eastern custom of removing his sandals. Overwhelmed with his own unworthiness in the divine presence, Moses hid his face lest he catch sight of the all-holy God.

Verses 7-10 reveal God's reasons for acting and they are a prelude for all God's actions that follow. God speaks continually in the first person singular and refers to Israel twice as "my people." God's relationship to them had already been rooted in the relationship with Abraham, Isaac, and Jacob. The verbs of 2:24-25 become more specific and intense: God has intensely seen the affliction of the people and God has personally heard their cry. God "knows" their suffering because God has intimately experienced their suffering. For God to "know" suffering means that the suffering has entered into the divine being so that God suffers with the people.

The freedom to be experienced in the event of Exodus is not just a freedom from oppression; it is also the freedom to live in a land of blessings and life. The good and spacious land of God's promise is the ultimate goal of Israel's deliverance. The "land flowing with milk and honey" is the first mention of what will be a frequent designation for the promised land in the Bible. It symbolizes fertility and abundance. The Canaanites, Hittites, etc. are the peoples occupying the land of Canaan at the time of the Israelite conquest.

All three traditions of God's revelation to Moses have been preserved by the editor. The Yahwist and Elohist traditions are woven together in these verses. In the Yahwist (vv. 7-8) God acts directly and personally, coming down to deliver Israel. In the Elohist (vv. 9-10) Moses is sent to bring the people out of Egypt. In the Yahwist, the personal name of God has been used since the beginning of Genesis, while the Elohist will recount the disclosure of the divine name. The Priestly tradition of Moses' commission is preserved in 6:2f.

Verse 11 begins a pattern of Moses' objections and God's reassurances. The final editor brings together the Yahwist and Elohist to show that neither God (v. 8) nor Moses (v. 10) act alone in bringing Israel to freedom. God takes the initiative in the dialogue, but it is clear that God needs Moses as the instrument of deliverance. Moses is not a passive recipient of God's will. His objections are taken seriously, and the give and take between God and Moses determines the shape of future events. Moses' reluctance, "Who am I?" is met by God's commitment, "I will be with you." Moses' lack of authority and ability is reinforced by the divine presence in the midst of the struggle. The prophetic sign of God's presence is that what Moses has experienced at Sinai will one day be the experience of all the children of Israel.

21

3:13-22 The Gift of God's Name

¹³"But," said Moses to God, "when I go to the Israelites and say to them, 'The God of your fathers has sent me to you,' if they ask me, 'What is his name?' what am I to tell them?" ¹⁴God replied, "I am who am." Then he added, "This is what you shall tell the Israelites: I AM sent me to you."

¹⁵God spoke further to Moses, "Thus shall you say to the Israelites: The Lord, the God of your fathers, the God of Abraham, the God of Isaac, the God of Jacob, has sent me to you.

"This is my name forever;
this is my title for all generations."

¹⁶"Go and assemble the elders of the Israelites, and tell them: The Lord, the God of your fathers, the God of Abraham, Isaac and Jacob, has appeared to me and said: I am concerned about you and about the way you are being treated in Egypt; ¹⁷so I have decided to lead you up out of the misery of Egypt into the land of the Canaanites, Hittites, Amorites, Perizzites, Hivites and Jebusites, a land flowing with milk and honey.

¹⁸"Thus they will heed your message. Then you and the elders of Israel shall go to the king of Egypt and say to him: The Lord, the God of the Hebrews, has sent us word. Permit us, then, to go a three-days' journey in the desert, that we may offer sacrifice to the Lord, our God.

¹⁹"Yet I know that the king of Egypt will not allow you to go unless he is forced. ²⁰I will stretch out my hand, therefore, and smite Egypt by doing all kinds of wondrous deeds there. After that he will send you away. ²¹I will even make the Egyptians so well-disposed toward this people that, when you leave, you will not go empty-handed. ²²Every woman shall ask her neighbor and her house guest for silver and gold articles and for clothing to put on your sons and daughters. Thus you will despoil the Egyptians."

Unlike our society in which a name is often only a label, in the ancient Near East a name expressed one's true nature. To know a divine name meant that one could call on the presence of the deity and create a relationship. Without a name, a god remained a distant impersonal force. For Israel, the gift of God's name was the revelation of the divine Person.

The Elohist tradition emphasizes that God's revelation of the divine name to Moses brings a newer and fuller understanding of who God is than was known to Israel's ancestors. God's truest nature is being revealed through the divine action of overthrowing oppressors and calling Israel to a new life characterized by freedom.

"Ehyeh-Asher-Ehyeh" has been translated in countless ways. The root verb conveys the idea of dynamic presence. "I will be who I will be," "I will cause to be what I will cause to be," and "I shall be there, as who I am, I shall be there" are all possible translations of God's enigmatic words. The phrase expresses the fullness and the mystery of God and, therefore, is left open to a wide range of interpretations.

The divine name consists of four Hebrew letters YHWH, sometimes called the sacred *Tetragrammaton*. Later centuries regarded the name as being so holy it was never pronounced. Whenever YHWH appeared in the biblical text, the reader would substitute the divine title *Adonai*, meaning "Lord." Unfortunately, the Greek translation and most modern translations also follow this practice and render YHWH as "The Lord." *Jehovah* is a mistaken pronunciation created by combining the Hebrew consonants and the vowels of the Hebrew *Adonai*.

The divine name is an expression of God's freedom. It does not express God as static and unchanging being, as western theology has often interpreted the name. Rather, it expresses the fact that the divine saving presence is always the result of God's freely-willed initiative. There are no limits to God's freedom to be present wherever and whenever God wills. The presence and power of Yahweh cannot be captured or controlled by building a temple, creating an idol, or invoking the right name, as was possible with other gods. God's name would only be understood as its meaning was unfolded in Israel's own historical experiences of God's dynamic presence with them. It is to share in this divine freedom that Israel is ultimately called.

4:1-9 Confirmation of Moses' Mission

[1]"But," objected Moses, "suppose they will not believe me, nor listen to my plea?" For they may say, 'The Lord did not appear to you.' " [2]The Lord therefore asked him, "What is that in your hand?" "A staff," he answered. [3]The Lord then said, "Throw it on the ground." When he threw it on the ground it was changed into a serpent, and Moses shied away from it. [4]"Now, put out your hand," the Lord said to him, "and take hold of its tail." So he put out his hand and laid hold of it, and it became a staff in his hand. [5]"This will take place so that they may believe," he continued, "that the Lord, the God of their fathers, the God of Abraham, the God of Isaac, the God of Jacob, did appear to you."

⁶Again the LORD said to him, "Put your hand in your bosom." He put it in his bosom, and when he withdrew it, to his surprise his hand was leprous, like snow. ⁷The LORD then said, "Now, put your hand back in your bosom." Moses put his hand back in his bosom, and when he withdrew it, to his surprise it was again like the rest of his body. ⁸"If they will not believe you, nor heed the message of the first sign, they should believe the message of the second. ⁹And if they will not believe even these two signs, nor heed your plea, take some water from the river and pour it on the dry land. The water you take from the river will become blood on the dry land."

In 3:18 God had assured Moses that Israel would heed his message. Yet, Moses does not at all share this divine certainty in his success. This dialogue with God revolves around a five-fold use of the Hebrew verb meaning "believe, trust." Moses' message to the Israelites in Egypt will be believed or not believed based on the confidence they have in the messenger. Moses feels the people will not believe him because they have no basis for trusting him. God takes seriously the objections of Moses and modifies the divine certainty with a series of conditional sentences in verses 8 and 9: "If they will not believe you . . . if they will not believe even these two signs . . . ." Disbelief in the prophets' message is characteristic of Israel's response throughout its history.

The three signs God gives are intended as much for Moses as they are for the people. Though such wondrous feats seem strange to our modern sensibilities, magic and dazzling deeds abound in the literature of Egypt. Since this type of activity was familiar to Israel in their land of bondage, God acts through these magical deeds to reassure Moses and Israel.

In Egypt snakes were seen as divine creatures; while in Hebrew literature, the snake is usually associated with evil. The ability to manipulate the snake is a sign of God's authority working through Moses. Diseases of the skin are often a sign of God's judgment in Hebrew writings. Leprosy made a person ritually unclean and forced the person into seclusion from the community. The restoration of Moses' hand is again a sign of God's power at work. Finally, the transformation of the water of the Nile into blood prefigures the series of ten wondrous signs God will work through Moses among the Egyptians.

Ultimately, however, belief and trust cannot be compelled by signs, no matter how spectacular. Israel will heed the message of God only through their developing relationship with God as the divine presence is made known through their experience of liberation.

4:10-17 Aaron's Office as Assistant

> ¹⁰Moses, however, said to the LORD, "If you please, Lord, I have never been eloquent, neither in the past, nor recently, nor now that you have spoken to your servant; but I am slow of speech and tongue." ¹¹The LORD said to him, "Who gives one man speech and makes another deaf and dumb? Or who gives sight to one and makes another blind? Is it not I, the LORD? ¹²Go, then! It is I who will assist you in speaking and will teach you what you are to say." ¹³Yet he insisted, "If you please, LORD, send someone else!" ¹⁴Then the LORD became angry with Moses and said, "Have you not your brother, Aaron the Levite? I know that he is an eloquent speaker. Besides, he is now on his way to meet you. ¹⁵When he sees you, his heart will be glad. You are to speak to him, then, and put the words in his mouth. I will assist both you and him in speaking and will teach the two of you what you are to do. ¹⁶He shall speak to the people for you: he shall be your spokesman, and you shall be as God to him. ¹⁷Take this staff in your hand; with it you are to perform the signs."

Again Moses protests God's call by claiming he does not speak well. Again God assures Moses that his own inadequacies do not matter because God's presence is with him. God, who gives the ability to see and hear and speak, will work through his impediments and enable Moses to use his gifts to manifest the divine will.

Running out of excuses, Moses finally asks God to choose someone else. At last we realize that Moses' deepest reluctance lay in his unwillingness to take responsibility and his desire to pass it on to someone else. Because God had patiently encouraged Moses through each objection and Moses still refused to accept the call, God became angry.

Verses 13-16 are of a secondary nature, subsequently inserted into the narrative. Aaron is to serve as the mouth of Moses, to speak his words, as a prophet does for God. Though this arrangement is not God's original intention, God accepts it as the next-best option. Moses remains central to God's plan, and in fact, the role of Aaron diminishes as the narrative progresses.

The staff is a sign of God's active presence and the divine authority given to Moses. It represents the "hand" of God and thus prepares the reader for the liberating events to come.

4:18-31 Moses' Return to Egypt

¹⁸After this Moses returned to his father-in-law Jethro and said to him, "Let me go back, please, to my kinsmen in Egypt, to see whether they are still living." Jethro replied, "Go in peace." ¹⁹In Midian the LORD said to Moses, "Go back to Egypt, for all the men who sought your life are dead." ²⁰So Moses took his wife and his sons, and started back to the land of Egypt, with them riding the ass. The staff of God he carried with him. ²¹The LORD said to him, "On your return to Egypt, see that you perform before Pharaoh all the wonders I have put in your power. I will make him obstinate, however, so that he will not let the people go. ²²So you shall say to Pharaoh: Thus says the LORD: Israel is my son, my first-born. ²³Hence I tell you: Let my son go, that he may serve me. If you refuse to let him go, I warn you, I will kill your son, your first-born."

²⁴On the journey, at a place where they spent the night, the LORD came upon Moses and would have killed him. ²⁵But Zipporah took a piece of flint and cut off her son's foreskin and, touching his person, she said, "You are a spouse of blood to me." ²⁶Then God let Moses go. At that time she said, "A spouse of blood," in regard to the circumcision.

²⁷The LORD said to Aaron, "Go into the desert to meet Moses." So he went, and when they met at the mountain of God, Aaron kissed him. ²⁸Moses informed him of all the LORD had said in sending him, and of the various signs he had enjoined upon him. ²⁹Then Moses and Aaron went and assembled all the elders of the Israelites. ³⁰Aaron told them everything the LORD had said to Moses, and he performed the signs before the people. ³¹The people believed, and when they heard that the LORD was concerned about them and had seen their affliction, they bowed down in worship.

This somewhat loosely joined series of events is bound together by the return of Moses from Midian to Egypt. Moses' reason for wanting to return to his kinsmen in Egypt, "to see whether they are still living," is an indication of the passage of time and the severity of their oppression. When Jethro raises no objections to Moses' departure, God assures Moses that there is no one left in Egypt who is seeking his life. Moses takes his wife and sons from their life in Midian, and he takes the "staff of God," prefiguring the new life of God's children which will be accomplished through the deeds of Yahweh.

The bond with Israel suggested here by God evokes all the intimacy of the parent-child relationship. God's relationship with Israel cannot be described only in juridical terminology, but it is a covenant of intimate love. God as parent enters deeply into the pains of the suffering child to bring it freedom and life. Israel is described as God's "firstborn" son. It implies that all people are in some way children of God, yet Israel has been chosen to receive the blessings of the firstborn. Within Israel, it was the firstborn sons who were said to belong to God in a special way. The text draws an exact parallel between God's firstborn son and Pharaoh's firstborn son. The death of Pharaoh's firstborn will show that he is an overlord who brings slavery and death rather than a parent who brings freedom and life.

Verses 24-26 are among the book's most obscure. It is probable that Moses, due to the abnormal circumstances of his infancy, had not been circumcised. While the family was on their journey God threatened the life of Moses because he could not be the leader of God's people unless this serious omission had been remedied. Acting quickly, Zipporah circumcised her son and then quickly daubed the genitals of Moses with the bloody foreskin. The act was a vicarious circumcision on behalf of Moses which averted the anger of God. The phrase "a spouse of blood" recalls that originally circumcision was a rite of puberty and a preparation for marriage. The words may be part of an ancient formula used in the marriage ritual.

Again it is a woman who saves Moses from death. Like the midwives, the mother and sister of Moses, and the daughter of Pharaoh, Zipporah's insight was instrumental in preserving God's plan for Israel. When God saw the blood and heard Zipporah's words the threat of death subsided. The event prefigures the night of Passover when, seeing the blood touched to the lintel and the doorposts, God will turn away the destroyer from the firstborn sons and bring Israel into life.

When Moses and Aaron spoke to the people of Israel, they believed. Yet, it is the words and the signs of God, not Moses and Aaron, that ground their belief. Their belief leads to worship when they hear that God has seen their affliction and is actively concerned about them. The next time the people will bow down in worship will be the night of Passover when God will save their life and deliver them from bondage.

5:1-13 Pharaoh's Obduracy

¹After that, Moses and Aaron went to Pharaoh and said, "Thus says the LORD, the God of Israel: Let my people go, that they may celebrate a feast to me in the desert." ²Pharaoh answered, "Who

is the LORD, that I should heed his plea to let Israel go? I do not know the LORD; even if I did, I would not let Israel go." ³They replied, "The God of the Hebrews has sent us word. Let us go a three days' journey in the desert, that we may offer sacrifice to the LORD, our God; otherwise he will punish us with pestilence or the sword."

⁴The king of Egypt answered them, "What do you mean, Moses and Aaron, by taking the people away from their work? Off to your labor! ⁵Look how numerous the people of the land are already," continued Pharaoh, "and yet you would give them rest from their labor!"

⁶That very day Pharaoh gave the taskmasters and foremen of the people this order: ⁷"You shall no longer supply the people with straw for their brickmaking as you have previously done. Let them go and gather straw themselves! ⁸Yet you shall levy upon them the same quota of bricks as they have previously made. Do not reduce it. They are lazy; that is why they are crying, 'Let us go to offer sacrifice to our God.' ⁹Increase the work for the men, so that they keep their mind on it and pay no attention to lying words."

¹⁰So the taskmasters and foremen of the people went out and told them, "Thus says Pharaoh: I will not provide you with straw. ¹¹Go and gather the straw yourselves, wherever you can find it. Yet there must not be the slightest reduction in your work." ¹²The people, then, scattered throughout the land of Egypt to gather stubble for straw, ¹³while the taskmasters kept driving them on, saying, "Finish your work, the same daily amount as when your straw was supplied."

   This unified section consists of several scenes depicting the dynamics of human oppression. The Egyptian pyramid forms the symbol of this oppressive system in which the few at the top benefit from the labor of the many at the bottom. The key is to keep those in bondage busy so that they do not have the time or the energy to complain. Any organized resistance must be met with harsher oppression. Giving in to any requests by those in bondage would be a sign of weakness.

   Moses' first approach to Pharaoh is confident and dramatic. Pharaoh's response is decisive and unyielding. The bitter conflict is set up between the lord of Egypt and the God of Israel. Pharaoh's question, "Who is Yahweh (the LORD)?" will be continually answered throughout the narrative. God's very name suggests that the identity of Israel's God will become known both to Pharaoh and to Israel as events progress. Whether Israel will serve Pharaoh or Yahweh becomes the overriding question of the narrative.

The second scene (vv. 6-9) shows Pharaoh moving to make Israel's conditions even worse. The oppression is intensified in order to prevent the people from reflecting on their situation. Any idol thoughts about shifting allegiance to anyone but Pharaoh must be crushed. His charge that the people are lazy is one of many tactics designed to shift the blame from the oppressor to the oppressed.

The third scene (vv. 10-13) communicates Pharaoh's response to the Israelites. Straw was a necessary ingredient for Egyptian brickmaking. Now the Israelites were commanded to hunt for stubble to add to the wet clay, while their production schedule for the mud bricks was kept the same. The words of the taskmasters, "Thus says Pharaoh. . . ." echoes the words of Moses and Aaron in verse 1, "Thus says the Lord." The unreasonable command increases the sense of hopelessness among the Israelites and leaves their spirits crushed. The protracted confrontation between the will of Pharaoh and that of Yahweh continues.

5:14-21 Complaint of the Foremen

¹⁴The foremen of the Israelites, whom the taskmasters of Pharaoh had placed over them, were beaten, and were asked, "Why have you not completed your prescribed amount of bricks yesterday and today, as before?"

¹⁵Then the Israelite foremen came and made this appeal to Pharaoh: "Why do you treat your servants in this manner? ¹⁶No straw is supplied to your servants, and still we are told to make bricks. Look how your servants are beaten! It is you who are at fault." ¹⁷Pharaoh answered, "It is just because you are lazy that you keep saying, 'Let us go and offer sacrifice to the Lord.' ¹⁸Off to work, then! Straw shall not be provided for you, but you must still deliver your quota of bricks."

¹⁹The Israelite foremen knew they were in a sorry plight, having been told not to reduce the daily amount of bricks. ²⁰When, therefore, they left Pharaoh and came upon Moses and Aaron, who were waiting to meet them, ²¹they said to them, "The Lord look upon you and judge! You have brought us into bad odor with Pharaoh and his servants and have put a sword in their hands to slay us."

Pharaoh's bureaucracy consisted of the Egyptian "taskmasters" who were higher officials and the "foremen" who were Hebrew bosses overseeing sections of workers. The Egyptians dealt directly with the foremen, who supervised the Hebrew laborers. Pharaoh enforced his will by creating these Israelite foremen who participated and collaborated in the system of exploitation. Yet, even they realize that their privileges last only as long as they can satisfy the demands of Pharaoh.

The fourth scene of this sequence (vv. 15-18) shows the foremen approaching Pharaoh. They come with the same bold confidence which we saw in the first scene with Moses and Aaron. Yet, the unyielding response of Pharaoh quickly leads to their discouragement. He responds again by declaring the Hebrews "lazy" and reaffirms his order to maintain the quota.

The fifth scene (vv. 19-21) demonstrates the clear results of the oppressor's tactics. The foremen turn on their own leaders, laying the blame on Moses and Aaron. Pharaoh has caused the people to believe that those seeking to liberate them are actually making the oppression much worse. He has divided and conquered, causing the Israelites to fight among themselves.

The final scene of chapter five (vv. 22-23) demonstrates the worst results of the oppressive system. As the foremen turned on Moses and accused him of the people's problems, Moses turns on God and accuses him. Now God is to blame as much as Pharaoh for the maltreatment of the Israelites. It is just a small step from here to the distorted belief among captive people that suffering and hardship is God's will.

5:22–6:13 Renewal of God's Promise

²²Moses again had recourse to the LORD and said, "LORD, why do you treat this people so badly? And why did you send me on such a mission? ²³Ever since I went to Pharaoh to speak in your name, he has maltreated this people of yours, and you have done nothing to rescue them."

6 ¹Then the LORD answered Moses, "Now you shall see what I will do to Pharaoh. Forced by my mighty hand, he will send them away; compelled by my outstretched arm, he will drive them from his land."

²God also said to Moses, "I am the LORD. ³As God the Almighty I appeared to Abraham, Isaac and Jacob, but my name, LORD, I did not make known to them. ⁴I also established my covenant with them, to give them the land of Canaan, the land in which they

were living as aliens. ⁵And now that I have heard the groaning of the Israelites, whom the Egyptians are treating as slaves, I am mindful of my covenant. ⁶Therefore, say to the Israelites: I am the LORD. I will free you from the forced labor of the Egyptians and will deliver you from their slavery. I will rescue you by my out-stretched arm and with mighty acts of judgment. ⁷I will take you as my own people, and you shall have me as your God. You will know that I, the LORD, am your God when I free you from the labor of the Egyptians ⁸and bring you into the land which I swore to give to Abraham, Isaac and Jacob. I will give it to you as your own possession—I, the LORD!" ⁹But when Moses told this to the Israelites, they would not listen to him because of their dejection and hard slavery.

¹⁰Then the LORD said to Moses, ¹¹"Go and tell Pharaoh, king of Egypt, to let the Israelites leave his land." ¹²But Moses protested to the LORD, "If the Israelites would not listen to me, how can it be that Pharaoh will listen to me, poor speaker that I am!" ¹³Still, the LORD, to bring the Israelites out of Egypt, spoke to Moses and Aaron and gave them his orders regarding both the Israelites and Pharaoh, king of Egypt.

The utter frustration and hopelessness presented in chapter 5 prepare for a renewed statement of God's saving resolve in chapter 6. From the point of view of Moses, God's plan had failed. Moses' mission had only made the condition of God's people worse. Yet, Moses' angry protest is met with understanding and new assurances from God.

There are many similarities between the account in 6:2-13 and the call to Moses at the burning bush. God is identified as the God of Israel's ancestors; Moses is assured that God has heard the cries of the Israelites; God promises to bring them out of slavery; God's promises are linked to the divine name; and Moses doubts whether he will be heeded by the people. This has led most scholars to acknowledge that these verses are another version of the call of God to Moses.

The account has many elements of the Priestly tradition. Written during the later period of Israel's exile in Babylon, this source is interested in demonstrating that God still saves Israel from bondage. The priestly tradition emphasizes that the relationship which God established with Israel's patriarchs is still active. Because God's faithfulness is everlasting, God freed Israel from Egypt and will free them also from Babylon.

In the priestly account, God does not "come down," nor is the divine presence shown through dramatic signs. The exchange between

God and Moses is minimized and the time and place of the exchange becomes irrelevant. God's covenant with Israel becomes all-important as God's promises of freedom and life made long ago are now linked to God's present action in the struggles of the people.

"I am Yahweh (the Lord)" is repeated four times like a refrain. It expresses the authority of God, present and active in history. God had previously been known as "El Shaddai (God the Almighty)" to Abraham and his descendants. This same God of Israel's ancestors is now dynamically present, calling the people of the covenant to freedom.

The heart of Yahweh's covenant promises are expressed here. Several verbs in verse 6 express God's saving action: "I will free you . . . deliver you . . . rescue you." The very heart of the covenant is expressed in verse 7: "I will take you as my own people, and you shall have me as your God." This relationship will be most fully realized when the Israelites are freed from oppression and brought into the land promised to their ancestors.

6:14-27 Genealogy of Moses and Aaron

[14]These are the heads of the ancestral houses. The sons of Reuben, the firstborn of Israel, were Hanoch, Pallu, Hezron and Carmi; these are the clans of Reuben. [15]The sons of Simeon were Jemuel, Jamin, Ohad, Jachin, Zohar and Shaul, who was the son of a Canaanite woman; these are the clans of Simeon. [16]The names of the sons of Levi, in their genealogical order, are Gershon, Kohath and Merari. Levi lived one hundred and thirty-seven years.

[17]The sons of Gershon, as heads of clans, were Libni and Shimei. [18]The sons of Kohath were Amram, Izhar, Hebron and Uzziel. Kohath lived one hundred and thirty-three years. [19]The sons of Merari were Mahli and Mushi. These are the clans of Levi in their genealogical order.

[20]Amram married his aunt Jochebed, who bore him Aaron, Moses and Miriam. Amram lived one hundred and thirty-seven years. [21]The sons of Izhar were Korah, Nepheg and Zichri. [22]The sons of Uzziel were Mishael, Elzaphan and Sithri. [23]Aaron married Amminadab's daughter, Elisheba, the sister of Nahshon; she bore him Nadab, Abihu, Eleazar and Ithamar. [24]The sons of Korah were Assir, Elkanah and Abiasaph. These are the clans of the Korahites. [25]Aaron's son, Eleazar, married one of Putiel's daughters, who bore him Phinehas. These are the heads of the ancestral clans of the Levites. [26]This is the Aaron and this the Moses to whom

the LORD said, "Lead the Israelites from the land of Egypt, company by company." ²⁷These are the ones who spoke to Pharaoh, king of Egypt, to bring the Israelites out of Egypt—the same Moses and Aaron.

The genealogy has been inserted into the narrative by the priestly writers. In the overall scheme of the narrative, it serves to link Moses and Aaron to the roots of Israel's ancient history. The first three sons of Jacob/Israel are listed—Reuben, Simeon, and Levi—along with their sons. Then the descendancy of Levi is listed: his eight grandsons and some of his great-grandsons. Aaron, Moses, and Miriam are listed as the children of Amram and Jochebed.

The principal concern of the priestly writers was to legitimate the role of Aaron by demonstrating his descendancy from the priestly lineage of Levi. While the importance of Moses needed no justification during the work's final editing, the priestly editors sought to authenticate Aaron as a worthy partner in the momentous events in Egypt. The genealogy does not include the family of Moses, but continues with Aaron's wife, four of his sons, one of his grandsons, and three sons of his cousin Qorach. Aaron is shown to be the ancestor of the legitimate priesthood at the time the priestly circle was setting Israel's tradition in writing.

The purpose of the genealogy is made clear as it is tied back into the narrative with verse 26. "This is the Aaron and this the Moses . . . ." to whom Yahweh spoke and who spoke to Pharaoh.

6:28–7:7 Moses and Aaron before Pharaoh

²⁸On the day the LORD spoke to Moses in Egypt ²⁹he said, "I am the LORD. Repeat to Pharaoh, king of Egypt, all that I tell you." ³⁰But Moses protested to the LORD, "Since I am a poor speaker, how can it be that Pharaoh will listen to me?"

7 ¹The LORD answered him, "See! I have made you as God to Pharaoh, and Aaron your brother shall act as your prophet. ²You shall tell him all that I command you. In turn, your brother Aaron shall tell Pharaoh to let the Israelites leave his land. ³Yet I will make Pharaoh so obstinate that, despite the many signs and wonders that I will work in the land of Egypt, ⁴he will not listen to you. Therefore I will lay my hand on Egypt and by great acts of judgment I will bring the hosts of my people, the Israelites, out of the land of Egypt, ⁵so that the Egyptians may learn that I am

33

the LORD, as I stretch out my hand against Egypt and lead the Israelites out of their midst."
⁶Moses and Aaron did as the LORD had commanded them. ⁷Moses was eighty years old and Aaron eighty-three when they spoke to Pharaoh.

As the call to Moses continues, the narrative gives a summary of what has occurred and a preview of what is to come. God's words tell us what is to happen, the ten plagues and the release of the Israelites from Egypt, and the meaning of these events in advance.

Moses' question about his own incompetence leads to God's assertion that Moses is but an instrument of God's actions. The role of Moses is to speak what Yahweh speaks. Aaron, in turn, is to communicate that divine word to Pharaoh as a prophet would speak for God.

Moses is correct in assuming that Pharaoh will be impassive toward him. Despite Moses' and Aaron's speaking God's commands, the resistance of Pharaoh will increase. The ruling pride of Pharaoh and the Egyptians and the hesitancy of Moses and the conquered slaves will grow. The obstinacy of Pharaoh will allow the "signs and wonders" to multiply, thus increasing their final impact.

The stubborn and inflexible will of Pharaoh is expressed literally in Hebrew as Pharaoh's "hardness of heart." This metaphor recurs no less than twenty times throughout these chapters. The continual refrain heightens the drama as the tyrannical will of Pharaoh is pitted against the relentless will of Yahweh to set people free.

God's will is ultimately intended not only to bring the Hebrews to freedom, but to bring the Egyptians to a knowledge of Yahweh. They must come to know that the God of freedom and life will not tolerate such attempts to crush the human spirit. The obstinacy of Pharaoh will bring the liberating movement of Yahweh to such a climax that even the Egyptians will experience and know the power of Israel's God.

Israel's tradition divides the life of Moses into three generations of forty years each. The first phase of life ended when he left Egypt for Midian (Acts 7:23); the second ended when he left Egypt; and the third ended after Israel's forty years in the wilderness (Deut 34:7). The notation that Moses was eighty years old and Aaron was three and eighty years marks an important transition in the history of Israel.

7:8-13 The Staff Turned into a Snake

⁸The LORD told Moses and Aaron, ⁹"If Pharaoh demands that you work a sign or wonder, you shall say to Aaron: Take your staff and throw it down before Pharaoh, and it will be changed into a snake." ¹⁰Then Moses and Aaron went to Pharaoh and did as the LORD had commanded. Aaron threw his staff down before Pharaoh and his servants, and it was changed into a snake. ¹¹Pharaoh, in turn, summoned wise men and sorcerers, and they also, the magicians of Egypt, did likewise by their magic arts. ¹²Each one threw down his staff, and it was changed into a snake. But Aaron's staff swallowed their staffs. ¹³Pharaoh, however, was obstinate and would not listen to them, just as the LORD had foretold.

This encounter of Moses and Aaron with Pharaoh prepares for all that will follow. The conflict is established between Yahweh and his servants, Moses and Aaron, and Pharaoh and his servants, the wise men and sorcerers. Ironically it is Pharaoh who demands to see a sign or wonder. God will grant his request many times over in the series of signs and wonders to come.

The Hebrew word used here for serpent (*tannin*) is different from that used in 4:3 (*nahas*). The creature in this passage is more terrifying than a common snake. In other biblical passages the word is often translated as "dragon" or "sea-monster" (Ps 74:13; Isa 51:9; Ezek 29:3). The word suggests the primordial powers of chaos and death that roam the sea. It is this threatening power that Yahweh will defeat in the Exodus.

The swallowing of the staff of all the Egyptian magicians is a sign of coming events. The only other use of the verb "swallow" in Exodus is in 15:12, referring to the swallowing of the Egyptians in the sea. Just as the staff of Aaron, representing the powerful hand of God, swallowed the powers of Egypt, so it is the right hand of God which will cause the waters to swallow their armies.

7:14-24 First Plague: Water Turned into Blood

¹⁴Then the LORD said to Moses, "Pharaoh is obdurate in refusing to let the people go. ¹⁵Tomorrow morning, when he sets out for the water, go and present yourself by the river bank, holding in your hand the staff that turned into a serpent. ¹⁶Say to him: The LORD, the God of the Hebrews, sent me to you with the message: Let my people go to worship me in the desert. But as yet you have

not listened. [17]The LORD now says: This is how you shall know that I am the LORD. I will strike the water of the river with the staff I hold, and it shall be changed into blood. [18]The fish in the river shall die, and the river itself shall become so polluted that the Egyptians will be unable to drink its water."

[19]The LORD then said to Moses, "Say to Aaron: Take your staff and stretch out your hand over the waters of Egypt—their streams and canals and pools, all their supplies of water—that they may become blood. Throughout the land of Egypt there shall be blood, even in the wooden pails and stone jars."

[20]Moses and Aaron did as the LORD had commanded. Aaron raised his staff and struck the waters of the river in full view of Pharaoh and his servants, and all the water of the river was changed into blood. [21]The fish in the river died, and the river itself became so polluted that the Egyptians could not drink its water. There was blood throughout the land of Egypt. [22]But the Egyptian magicians did the same by their magic arts. So Pharaoh remained obstinate and would not listen to Moses and Aaron, just as the LORD had foretold. [23]He turned away and went into his house, with no concern even for this. [24]All the Egyptians had to dig in the neighborhood of the river for drinking water, since they could not drink the river water.

The account of the ten plagues, like most of the Exodus narrative, is told in epic form. Events that were much more complex in their historical reality are narrated in dramatic and broadly sweeping strokes. The narrators were not interested in merely handing down information about the past. Rather, they wanted to proclaim what Yahweh had done for them and to declare their understanding of the essential meaning of these events. By simplifying and overstating the historical reality, they announced the wondrous nature of God at work on their behalf.

Much has been made of the question of whether the plagues were miraculous events or strictly natural phenomena. However, such a question was quite foreign to the mentality of the Israelite people. A number of the plagues do seem to be related to phenomena which occasionally occur in Egypt: destructive hailstorms, locust swarms, and dusty winds that darken the skies for days. However, what is emphasized by the memory of the Israelites is the fact that the hand of God did these things in order to free them and that only a closed heart could fail to understand.

It is clear that in the course of centuries of oral transmission various traditions told the story of the plagues quite differently. Though the final edited version of the plagues is a masterful narrative, there are many hints that it is a compilation of several sources. The final redactor joined together varying traditions without always eliminating inconsistencies.

The earliest tradition, the Yahwist, told of seven plagues. It seems that the author of Psalm 78 was familiar only with the Yahwist tradition as it recounts only the seven plagues of the early source, though in a different order. In its characteristic lively style, the Yahwist authors introduce each plague with an exchange between Moses and Yahweh, then between Moses and Pharaoh. Yahweh sends Moses to Pharaoh with the message: "Thus says the LORD: Let my people go to worship me." Moses then announces the plague and Yahweh alone brings it about. Pharaoh, seeing the effects of the plague, then asks for Moses to intercede for the plague's removal. After seeming to have a concession from Pharaoh to free the people, Yahweh lifts the plague, but Pharaoh's heart is still hard and he refuses to let the Israelites leave.

The latest tradition, the Priestly, differs from the above in several of its features. The most obvious distinction is the major role played by Aaron in all the action. He stretches out his staff to bring on the plague. The magicians play an important role as allies of Pharaoh. Generally the priestly source tends to be less detailed but more spectacular in its descriptions. It emphasizes that everything happens in fulfillment of the powerful word of Yahweh.

By combining elements of these two traditions, and possibly also elements of the Elohist tradition, the Priestly editors fixed the number of the plagues at ten. This is a convenient number in the Israelite tradition for teaching lists to future generations, since ten is ideal for counting on the fingers.

The account of the first plague indicates the sometimes uneven combination of these different sources. The Yahwist source declares that the plague was brought about directly by Yahweh (v. 17a, 18); the Elohist source indicates it was the staff of Moses (v. 15); and the Priestly source declares it was the staff of Aaron (v. 19). The Yahwist source indicates that the Nile was turned to blood, while the Priestly source adds that every bit of water in Egypt was turned to blood.

The plagues show how the elements of the created world become sources of destruction when they are distorted by the powers of bondage and death. The waters of the Nile were the constant source of life and renewal for the land of Egypt, yet they become a destructive power under Pharaoh's plan. Blood was the basic element of life and will be a sign of liberation for Israel at the Passover. Yet, the bloody Nile foreshadows the destruction that will be brought upon the Egyptians when they meet their death in the waters of the sea, and the "blood throughout the land of Egypt" foreshadows the final plague where death will be visited on every house in Egypt.

7:25–8:11 Second Plague: the Frogs

²⁵Seven days passed after the LORD had struck the river. ²⁶Then the LORD said to Moses, "Go to Pharaoh and tell him: Thus says the LORD: Let my people go to worship me. ²⁷If you refuse to let them go, I warn you, I will send a plague of frogs over all your territory. ²⁸The river will teem with frogs. They will come up into your palace and into your bedroom and onto your bed, into the houses of your servants, too, and your subjects, even into your ovens and your kneading bowls. ²⁹The frogs will swarm all over you and your subjects and your servants."

8 ¹The LORD then told Moses, "Say to Aaron: Stretch out your hand and your staff over the streams and canals and pools, to make frogs overrun the land of Egypt." ²Aaron stretched out his hand over the waters of Egypt, and the frogs came up and covered the land of Egypt. ³But the magicians did the same by their magic arts. They, too, made frogs overrun the land of Egypt.

⁴Then Pharaoh summoned Moses and Aaron and said, "Pray the LORD to remove the frogs from me and my subjects, and I will let the people go to offer sacrifice to the LORD." ⁵Moses answered Pharaoh, "Do me the favor of appointing the time when I am to pray for you and your servants and your subjects, that the frogs may be taken away from you and your houses and be left only in the river." ⁶"Tomorrow," said Pharaoh. Then Moses replied, "It shall be as you have said, so that you may learn that there is none like the LORD, our God. ⁷The frogs shall leave you and your houses, your servants and your subjects; only in the river shall they be left."

⁸After Moses and Aaron left Pharaoh's presence, Moses implored the LORD to fulfill the promise he had made to Pharaoh about the frogs; ⁹and the LORD did as Moses had asked. The frogs in the houses and courtyards and fields died off. ¹⁰Heaps and heaps of them were gathered up, and there was a stench in the land. ¹¹But when Pharaoh saw that there was a respite, he became obdurate and would not listen to them, just as the LORD had foretold.

The image of frogs swarming everywhere in Egypt—hopping and croaking in every home, in their ovens and cooking pots, and even entering into the palace of Pharaoh and invading his bed—was a delightfully humorous memory for the generations of Israelites who retold the story. Though Pharaoh was warned by Moses of the consequences of his continued stubbornness, he refused to let the people go.

The humor increases as the magicians of Egypt only copy what has been done by Moses and Aaron and thus make matters worse for Pharaoh. Rather than undoing the plague, they duplicate the already dreadful situation.

For the first time there is a change in Pharaoh's attitude. Using the name of Israel's God, he asks Moses and Aaron to pray to Yahweh for the removal of the frogs, adding that he will let the people go. There is at least the beginning of Pharaoh's acknowledgment of Yahweh whom he declared earlier not to know (5:2).

In order to further convince Pharaoh of the powers of Yahweh, Moses invited Pharaoh to name the time he is to pray for the removal of the plague. The death of the frogs throughout the houses and fields of Egypt becomes a subtle sign to Pharaoh. If he continues to harden his heart and continues to oppose the God of life, soon there will be dead from every household and from all the animals of the fields (12:29-30).

8:12-15 Third Plague: the Gnats

¹²Thereupon the LORD said to Moses, "Tell Aaron to stretch out his staff and strike the dust of the earth, that it may be turned into gnats throughout the land of Egypt." ¹³They did so. Aaron stretched out his hand, and with his staff he struck the dust of the earth, and gnats came upon man and beast. The dust of the earth was turned into gnats throughout the land of Egypt. ¹⁴Though the magicians tried to bring forth gnats by their magic arts, they could not do so. As the gnats infested man and beast, ¹⁵the magicians said to Pharaoh, "This is the finger of God." Yet Pharaoh remained obstinate and would not listen to them, just as the LORD had foretold.

The plague exemplifies the elements of the priestly tradition only. It is Aaron who effects the plague with his staff; the magicians attempt to duplicate the sign; and everything happened according to the word of Yahweh.

The thrice-repeated "dust," which becomes the gnats of the plague, is used throughout the Scriptures to refer to human mortality. Human beings come from dust, and to dust they return at death (Gen 3:19; Eccl 3:20). The image suggests the death of the Egyptians who ally themselves with the hardened heart of Pharaoh.

The new element in the narrative is the powerlessness of the magicians to replicate the deed. They declare that they have been outdistanced in this contest of power as they recognize the "finger" of God at work. Still Pharaoh refuses to take seriously the deeds of Moses and Aaron.

8:16-28 Fourth Plague: the Flies

[16]Again the LORD told Moses, "Early tomorrow morning present yourself to Pharaoh when he goes forth to the water, and say to him: Thus says the LORD: Let my people go to worship me. [17]If you will not let my people go, I warn you, I will loose swarms of flies upon you and your servants and your subjects and your houses. The houses of the Egyptians and the very ground on which they stand shall be filled with swarms of flies. [18]But on that day I will make an exception of the land of Goshen: there shall be no flies where my people dwell, that you may know that I am the LORD in the midst of the earth. [19]I will make this distinction between my people and your people. This sign shall take place tomorrow." [20]This the LORD did. Thick swarms of flies entered the house of Pharaoh and the houses of his servants; throughout Egypt the land was infested with flies.

[21]Then Pharaoh summoned Moses and Aaron and said to them, "Go and offer sacrifice to your God in this land." [22]But Moses replied, "It is not right to do so, for the sacrifices we offer to the LORD, our God, are an abomination to the Egyptians. If before their very eyes we offer sacrifices which are an abomination to them, will not the Egyptians stone us? [23]We must go a three days' journey in the desert to offer sacrifice to the LORD, our God, as he commands us." [24]"Well, then," said Pharaoh, "I will let you go to offer sacrifice to the LORD, your God, in the desert, provided that you do not go too far away and that you pray for me." [25]Moses answered, "As soon as I leave your presence I will pray to the LORD that the flies may depart tomorrow from Pharaoh and his servants and his subjects. Pharaoh, however, must not play false again by refusing to let the people go to offer sacrifice to the LORD." [26]When Moses left Pharaoh's presence, he prayed to the LORD; [27]and the

LORD did as Moses had asked. He removed the flies from Pharaoh and his servants and subjects. Not one remained. ²⁸But once more Pharaoh became obdurate and would not let the people go.

The lively details of the plague, the direct dialogue of Yahweh with Moses, and Yahweh's singular action in bringing about the plague demonstrate the characteristics of the Yahwist tradition. The new element here is the distinction made by God between the Israelites and the Egyptians. The land of Goshen, in the eastern part of the delta where the Israelites were living, did not experience the swarms of flies. This distinction will continue and reach its climax when God definitively separates the Israelites from the Egyptians at the Passover.

An extended negotiation ensues between Moses and Pharaoh. Pharaoh agrees to let the Israelites offer sacrifice, but with the stipulation that it be "in this land." Moses' response that the sacrifices would be insulting to the Egyptians is accepted by Pharaoh who then allows them to go in the wilderness provided they do not go far. Moses accepts the compromise and is true to his word. Yet Pharaoh breaks his word—a response that the reader has come to expect.

9:1-7 Fifth Plague: the Pestilence

¹Then the LORD said to Moses, "Go to Pharaoh and tell him: Thus says the LORD, the God of the Hebrews: Let my people go to worship me. ²If you refuse to let them go and persist in holding them, ³I warn you, the LORD will afflict all your livestock in the field— your horses, asses, camels, herds and flocks—with a very severe pestilence. ⁴But the LORD will distinguish between the livestock of Israel and that of Egypt, so that none belonging to the Israelites will die." ⁵And setting a definite time, the LORD added, "Tomorrow the LORD shall do this in the land." ⁶And on the next day the LORD did so. All the livestock of the Egyptians died, but not one beast belonging to the Israelites. ⁷But though Pharaoh's messengers informed him that not even one beast belonging to the Israelites had died, he still remained obdurate and would not let the people go.

The severe pestilence increases the tension beyond the discomforting annoyances of the previous plagues to the death of all the Egyptian livestock. Unlike the previous Yahwist accounts, there is no negotiation between Yahweh and Pharaoh.

The distinction between the Egyptians and the Israelites, begun in the fourth plague, is further developed. Here Pharaoh sent his messenger to verify that Israel's livestock had all lived. The fact that the epidemic came with such sweeping devastation upon all the animals of Egypt, combined with the fact that not one of Israel's beasts had died, increases the reader's amazement at Pharaoh's stubbornness.

9:8-12 Sixth Plague: the Boils

⁸Then the LORD said to Moses and Aaron, "Take a double handful of soot from a furnace, and in the presence of Pharaoh let Moses scatter it toward the sky. ⁹It will then turn into fine dust over the whole land of Egypt and cause festering boils on man and beast throughout the land."

¹⁰So they took soot from a furnace and stood in the presence of Pharaoh. Moses scattered it toward the sky, and it caused festering boils on man and beast. ¹¹The magicians could not stand in Moses' presence, for there were boils on the magicians no less than on the rest of the Egyptians. ¹²But the LORD made Pharaoh obstinate, and he would not listen to them, just as the LORD had foretold to Moses.

The intensity of the plagues mounts as the festering boils afflict people and beasts alike. Though the passage displays all the other characteristics of the Priestly tradition, the plague is not brought about by the staff of Aaron, but through the scattering of the soot by Moses.

The magicians are not only unable to reproduce the plague, but they become its victims. Stripped of their powers and no longer able to compete with Moses, they disappear from the narrative.

9:13-35 Seventh Plague: the Hail

¹³Then the LORD told Moses, "Early tomorrow morning present yourself to Pharaoh and say to him: Thus says the LORD, the God of the Hebrews: Let my people go to worship me, ¹⁴or this time I will hurl all my blows upon you and your servants and your subjects, that you may know that there is none like me anywhere on earth. ¹⁵For by now I would have stretched out my hand and struck you and your subjects with such pestilence as would wipe you from the earth. ¹⁶But this is why I have spared you: to show you my power and to make my name resound throughout the earth! ¹⁷Will

you still block the way for my people by refusing to let them go? [18]I warn you, then, tomorrow at this hour I will rain down such fierce hail as there has never been in Egypt from the day the nation was founded up to the present. [19]Therefore, order all your livestock and whatever else you have in the open fields to be brought to a place of safety. Whatever man or beast remains in the fields and is not brought to shelter shall die when the hail comes upon them." [20]Some of Pharaoh's servants feared the warning of the LORD and hurried their servants and livestock off to shelter. [21]Others, however, did not take the warning of the LORD to heart and left their servants and livestock in the fields.

[22]The LORD then said to Moses, "Stretch out your hand toward the sky, that hail may fall upon the entire land of Egypt, on man and beast and every growing thing in the land of Egypt." [23]When Moses stretched out his staff toward the sky, the LORD sent forth hail and peals of thunder. Lightning flashed toward the earth, and the LORD rained down hail upon the land of Egypt; [24]and lightning constantly flashed through the hail, such fierce hail as had never been seen in the land since Egypt became a nation. [25]It struck down every man and beast that was in the open throughout the land of Egypt; it beat down every growing thing and splintered every tree in the fields. [26]Only in the land of Goshen, where the Israelites dwelt, was there no hail.

[27]Then Pharaoh summoned Moses and Aaron and said to them, "I have sinned again! The LORD is just; it is I and my subjects who are at fault. [28]Pray to the LORD, for we have had enough of God's thunder and hail. Then I will let you go; you need stay no longer." [29]Moses replied, "As soon as I leave the city I will extend my hands to the LORD; the thunder will cease, and there will be no more hail. Thus you shall learn that the earth is the LORD's. [30]But you and your servants, I know, do not yet fear the LORD God."

[31]Now the flax and the barley were ruined, because the barley was in ear and the flax in bud. [32]But the wheat and the spelt were not ruined, for they grow later.

[33]When Moses had left Pharaoh's presence and had gone out of the city, he extended his hands to the LORD. Then the thunder and the hail ceased, and the rain no longer poured down upon the earth. [34]But Pharaoh, seeing that the rain and hail and thunder had ceased, sinned again; he with his servants became obdurate, [35]and in his obstinacy he would not let the Israelites go, as the LORD had foretold through Moses.

Yahweh's warning is amplified as Pharaoh is told of the destruction and death that is to come. Though the divine power has been demonstrated mightily in the previous plagues, Yahweh has actually shown gracious restraint in prolonging the plagues. Rather than destroy Pharaoh, as his oppressive deeds deserve, God has a more comprehensive purpose: to show Pharaoh his power and to cause God's name to be declared throughout the earth. Since God's purpose is not destruction but deliverance, Pharaoh becomes an instrument of God's universal saving will.

There is evidence, for the first time, that God was having an influence over some of the Egyptians. Those who respected the word of Yahweh and took their servants and livestock to shelter were preserved from the effects of the hail, just as the Israelites living in Goshen were not touched by the devastation. Even Pharaoh, for the first time, acknowledged that he had sinned and that he and his subjects were at fault.

Not only is the hail destructive of animals and crops, but it results in the first Egyptian deaths. The devastating effects of the plague now extend to every form of life in Egypt. The intensity of the destruction prepares for the calamity to come in the final plagues, and the thunder and lightning prepare for the manifestations at Sinai.

10:1-20 Eighth Plague: the Locusts

¹Then the LORD said to Moses, "Go to Pharaoh, for I have made him and his servants obdurate in order that I may perform these signs of mine among them ²and that you may recount to your son and grandson how ruthlessly I dealt with the Egyptians and what signs I wrought among them, so that you may know that I am the LORD."

³So Moses and Aaron went to Pharaoh and told him, "Thus says the LORD, the God of the Hebrews: How long will you refuse to submit to me? Let my people go to worship me. ⁴If you refuse to let my people go, I warn you, tomorrow I will bring locusts into your country. ⁵They shall cover the ground, so that the ground itself will not be visible. They shall eat up the remnant you saved unhurt from the hail, as well as the foilage that has since sprouted in your fields. ⁶They shall fill your houses and the houses of your servants and of all the Egyptians; such a sight your fathers or grandfathers have not seen from the day they first settled on this soil up to the present day." With that he turned and left Pharaoh.

⁷But Pharaoh's servants said to him, "How long must he be a menace to us? Let the men go to worship the LORD, their God. Do you not yet realize that Egypt is being destroyed?" ⁸So Moses

and Aaron were brought back to Pharaoh, who said to them, "You may go and worship the Lord, your God. But how many of you will go?" ⁹"Young and old must go with us," Moses answered, "our sons and daughters as well as our flocks and herds must accompany us. That is what a feast of the Lord means to us." ¹⁰"The Lord help you," Pharaoh replied, "if I ever let your little ones go with you! Clearly, you have some evil in mind. ¹¹No, no! Just you men can go and worship the Lord. After all, that is what you want." With that they were driven from Pharaoh's presence.

¹²The Lord then said to Moses, "Stretch out your hand over the land of Egypt, that locusts may swarm over it and eat up all the vegetation and whatever the hail has left." ¹³So Moses stretched out his staff over the land of Egypt, and the Lord sent an east wind blowing over the land all that day and all that night. At dawn the east wind brought the locusts. ¹⁴They swarmed over the whole land of Egypt and settled down on every part of it. Never before had there been such a fierce swarm of locusts, nor will there ever be. ¹⁵They covered the surface of the whole land, till it was black with them. They ate up all the vegetation in the land and the fruit of whatever trees the hail had spared. Nothing green was left on any tree or plant throughout the land of Egypt.

¹⁶Hastily Pharaoh summoned Moses and Aaron and said, "I have sinned against the Lord, your God, and against you. ¹⁷But now, do forgive me my sin once more, and pray the Lord, your God, to take at least this deadly pest from me." ¹⁸When Moses left the presence of Pharaoh, he prayed to the Lord, ¹⁹and the Lord changed the wind to a very strong west wind, which took up the locusts and hurled them into the Red Sea. But though not a single locust remained within the confines of Egypt, ²⁰the Lord made Pharaoh obstinate, and he would not let the Israelites go.

The continuing reference to Pharaoh's hardened heart (obduracy) is stated here at the beginning of the plague in order to further explain God's purpose. The plagues continue not only so that the Egyptians may see Yahweh's power, but also so that Moses may recount the signs of God's saving presence among the future generations of Israelites. This oral transmission from generation to generation is the foundation of the written account and the root of the tradition connecting Moses with the narration of the Book of Exodus.

Moses was uncompromising in his negotiations with Pharaoh. When Pharaoh insisted that only the men would be allowed to go and worship God, thus insuring their return to their families in Egypt, Moses persistently demanded that all Israel, young and old, male and female, was called to participate in the pilgrimage-worship of Yahweh.

The vast expanse of the locust swarm, decimating the food supply of Egypt, threatens the life of all Egypt. The comprehensiveness of the destruction, portending mass starvation and jeopardizing the future of Egypt, brings Pharaoh from his previous arrogance to an attitude approaching penitence: "I have sinned . . . forgive me my sin . . . pray the LORD, your God . . . ."

The course of the plague presages the climactic events that will soon transpire. The east wind which brings the locusts is the same wind that will turn the sea into dry land allowing the Hebrews to cross. The end of the plague, marked by the opposite wind which hurled every locust into the sea so that not a single one remained, anticipates the wind which will cover the Egyptians so that not a single one will escape (14:28).

10:21-29 Ninth Plague: the Darkness

[21]Then the LORD said to Moses, "Stretch out your hand toward the sky, that over the land of Egypt there may be such intense darkness that one can feel it." [22]So Moses stretched out his hand toward the sky, and there was dense darkness throughout the land of Egypt for three days. [23]Men could not see one another, nor could they move from where they were, for three days. But all the Israelites had light where they dwelt.

[24]Pharaoh then summoned Moses and Aaron and said, "Go and worship the LORD. Your little ones, too, may go with you. But your flocks and herds must remain." [25]Moses replied, "You must also grant us sacrifices and holocausts to offer up to the LORD, our God. [26]Hence, our livestock also must go with us. Not an animal must be left behind. Some of them we must sacrifice to the LORD, our God, but we ourselves shall not know which ones we must sacrifice to him until we arrive at the place itself." [27]But the LORD made Pharaoh obstinate, and he would not let them go. [28]"Leave my presence," Pharaoh said to him, "and see to it that you do not appear before me again! The day you appear before me you shall die!" [29]Moses replied, "Well said! I will never appear before you again."

The darkness falls upon Egypt for three days without any warning for Pharaoh. The eternally rising sun was, for the Egyptians, the chief source of creative life. Following the previous two plagues that had destroyed all growth in the land, this darkness blocking out the sun threatens the Egyptians with total extinction. Described as a tangible and paralyzing darkness, it is the most fearful and ominous of the plagues to this point. The word describing the darkness, variously translated as "dense" or "eerie" suggests an impending cataclysm, the fearful gloom associated with God's judgment on the Day of Yahweh (Isa 8:22; Joel 2:2).

Pharaoh's final concession, to let all the Hebrews go without their livestock, is rejected by Moses. The section ends with a note of finality as Pharaoh responds in furious anger, threatening to put Moses to death if he ever sees him again. It is clear that negotiation has failed because of the stubborn heart of the oppressor and now the issue at stake is the complete freedom of the Israelites.

11:1-10 Tenth Plague: the Death of the First-born

¹Then the LORD told Moses, "One more plague will I bring upon Pharaoh and upon Egypt. After that he will let you depart. In fact, he will not merely let you go; he will drive you away. ²Instruct your people that every man is to ask his neighbor, and every woman her neighbor, for silver and gold articles and for clothing." ³The LORD indeed made the Egyptians well-disposed toward the people; Moses himself was very highly regarded by Pharaoh's servants and the people in the land of Egypt.

⁴Moses then said, "Thus says the LORD: At midnight I will go forth through Egypt. ⁵Every first-born in this land shall die, from the first-born of Pharaoh on the throne to the first-born of the slave-girl at the handmill, as well as all the first-born of the animals. ⁶Then there shall be loud wailing throughout the land of Egypt, such as has never been, nor will ever be again. ⁷But among the Israelites and their animals not even a dog shall growl, so that you may know how the LORD distinguishes between the Egyptians and the Israelites. ⁸All these servants of yours shall then come down to me, and prostrate before me, they shall beg me, 'Leave us, you and all your followers!' Only then will I depart." With that he left Pharaoh's presence in hot anger.

⁹The LORD said to Moses, "Pharaoh refuses to listen to you that my wonders may be multiplied in the land of Egypt." ¹⁰Thus, although Moses and Aaron performed these various wonders in Pharaoh's presence, the LORD made Pharaoh obstinate, and he would not let the Israelites leave his land.

This section provides a transition between the first nine plagues mediated by Moses and the events which form the heart of the Exodus. It brings what has gone before to a climax and lays the necessary foundation for the Passover event. The time for deliverance is at hand and there is no longer any allowance for dialogue with Pharaoh. Moses simply announces that the death of the first-born will take place and that it will lead to the Exodus.

Yahweh's solidarity with the Israelites continues to be demonstrated. God will cause the Egyptians to respond favorably to the Israelites' request for silver, gold, and clothing. Because of this plundering of Egypt's riches, the Israelites will leave Egypt as a victor would leave a battle. God's distinction between the two people is vividly demonstrated by the contrast between the anguished cries of the Egyptians and the undisturbed quiet within the Israelite settlement. The final separation will occur as the Egyptians, knowing the power of Yahweh and where the divine favor rests, bow before Moses and beg the Israelites to leave.

The ten plagues have demonstrated, both to the Egyptians and the Israelites, the nature of Yahweh as the God of freedom and life. The plagues happen because of the oppressive and life-threatening policies of Pharaoh which violate God's will for people's lives. The natural world and people become victims of such death-dealing powers. By restoring the Israelites to freedom, God will be able to move with this liberated people to extend the divine purpose for humanity to all the earth.

12:1-20 The Passover Ritual Prescribed

¹The LORD said to Moses and Aaron in the land of Egypt, ²"This month shall stand at the head of your calendar; you shall reckon it the first month of the year. ³Tell the whole community of Israel: On the tenth of this month every one of your families must procure for itself a lamb, one apiece for each household. ⁴If a family is too small for a whole lamb, it shall join the nearest household in procuring one and shall share in the lamb in proportion to the number of persons who partake of it. ⁵The lamb must be a year-old male and without blemish. You may take it from either the sheep or the goats. ⁶You shall keep it until the fourteenth day of this month, and then, with the whole assembly of Israel present, it shall be slaughtered during the evening twilight. ⁷They shall take some of its blood and apply it to the two doorposts and the lintel of every house in which they partake of the lamb. ⁸That same night they shall eat its roasted flesh with unleavened bread and bitter

herbs. ⁹It shall not be eaten raw or boiled, but roasted whole, with its head and shanks and inner organs. ¹⁰None of it must be kept beyond the next morning; whatever is left over in the morning shall be burned up.

¹¹"This is how you are to eat it: with your loins girt, sandals on your feet and your staff in hand, you shall eat like those who are in flight. It is the Passover of the LORD. ¹²For on this same night I will go through Egypt, striking down every first-born of the land, both man and beast, and executing judgment on all the gods of Egypt—I, the LORD! ¹³But the blood will mark the houses where you are. Seeing the blood, I will pass over you; thus, when I strike the land of Egypt, no destructive blow will come upon you.

¹⁴"This day shall be a memorial feast for you, which all your generations shall celebrate with pilgrimage to the LORD, as a perpetual institution. ¹⁵For seven days you must eat unleavened bread. From the very first day you shall have your houses clear of all leaven. Whoever eats leavened bread from the first day to the seventh shall be cut off from Israel. ¹⁶On the first day you shall hold a sacred assembly, and likewise on the seventh. On these days you shall not do any sort of work, except to prepare the food that everyone needs.

¹⁷"Keep, then, this custom of the unleavened bread. Since it was on this very day that I brought your ranks out of the land of Egypt, you must celebrate this day throughout your generations as a perpetual institution. ¹⁸From the evening of the fourteenth day of the first month until the evening of the twenty-first day of this month you shall eat unleavened bread. ¹⁹For seven days no leaven may be found in your houses. Anyone, be he a resident alien or a native, who eats leavened food shall be cut off from the community of Israel. ²⁰Nothing leavened may you eat; wherever you dwell you may eat only unleavened bread."

Just as Yahweh's redeeming action for the Israelites is about to come to a climax, the narrative pauses to introduce ritual instructions for commemorating what is about to take place. God's instructions for what the Israelites are to do on this particular night are joined with detailed prescriptions of how they are to celebrate Passover in the years to come. In fact, the way the ritual was celebrated in later years influenced the way the Exodus tradition was remembered and thus the form in which it comes to us in writing. The liturgy has shaped the literature.

The ritual celebration of Passover has a timeless quality. When the Israelites reenacted the Passover, it was not simply a recollection of a past event. As often as the Israelites commemorated this event down through the centuries, it always made the redeeming reality present for them. In the memorial feast the saving power of the past event became present again in the timeless moment of the ritual. It was as though all the past and future generations of Israel came together on this night of the Passover meal to be reconstituted as the people of God.

Instructions for the Passover liturgy are set forth in minute and elaborate detail. The month of the feast was to be at the head of the calendar because it marked the beginning of Israel's existence as a free people. The month was Abib (13:4), later called by its Babylonian name Nisan, approximately our March–April. Every family of Israel was to select a lamb on the tenth of the month and keep it until the fourteenth when it was to be slaughtered. The selected animal was to be a year-old male chosen with care. After smearing its blood on the doorposts and lintels of the house, the family was to roast the animal whole and eat it with an attitude of haste while dressed in traveling attire for departure.

Blood is the essential element of life. The blood of the lamb, marking the entrance to the homes of the Israelites, becomes the means of Israel's redemption. There is some evidence that this blood ritual predated the Israelite celebration and was originally a spring departure feast of Israel's nomadic ancestors. Dedicating the first-born of their flock to God, they would put the blood on their tent poles to drive away evil powers and procure fecundity for the flock before their journey. The new beginnings brought by the Passover caused Israel to give new meaning to this ancient rite.

Originally Passover and the Feast of Unleavened Bread were two separate feasts. While Passover was a nomadic observance, Unleavened Bread was an agricultural feast. It originally celebrated the first sheaves of the barley crop. Throughout the year, bread was baked by including a small piece of the leavened dough from the day before to provide the ferment. When the new barley crop was ready, the leaven from the previous year was cleared from all the houses as a sign of new beginnings. The bread made from the first grain of the year was to be eaten in its pure state without the admixture of ferment.

Since these two ancient feasts fell at the same time of year, they were united to form a week of remembrance of Israel's founding event. Beginning with the night of the first full moon of spring, all Israel celebrated the end of their bondage and their liberation to new life.

12:21-28 Promulgation of the Passover

²¹Moses called all the elders of Israel and said to them, "Go and procure lambs for your families, and slaughter them as Passover victims. ²²Then take a bunch of hyssop, and dipping it in the blood that is in the basin, sprinkle the lintel and the two doorposts with this blood. But none of you shall go outdoors until morning. ²³For the LORD will go by, striking down the Egyptians. Seeing the blood on the lintel and the two doorposts, the LORD will pass over that door and not let the destroyer come into your houses to strike you down.

²⁴"You shall observe this as a perpetual ordinance for yourselves and your descendants. ²⁵Thus, you must also observe this rite when you have entered the land which the LORD will give you as he promised. ²⁶When your children ask you, 'What does this rite of yours mean?' ²⁷you shall reply, 'This is the Passover sacrifice of the LORD, who passed over the houses of the Israelites in Egypt; when he struck down the Egyptians, he spared our houses.' "

Then the people bowed down in worship, ²⁸and the Israelites went and did as the LORD had commanded Moses and Aaron.

The instructions Yahweh has given to Moses are now transmitted to the people. Again liturgical directions are incorporated into the narrative material. No mention is made of the meal, since the focus here is Israel's protection from the deadly effects of the tenth plague. The blood ritual consists of sprinkling the lamb's blood on the lintel and doorposts with a bundle of hyssop. The entrance of each house then becomes the separation point between life and death, between Israelites and Egyptians.

The word "rite" in verses 25 and 26, referring to Israel's service of Yahweh, is the same Hebrew word used throughout the previous chapters to refer to their slave labor in the service of Pharaoh. The work done for Yahweh in freedom is graphically different in spirit than the work done for Pharaoh through the coercion of slavery.

The concern here is for an understanding of the ritual as it is continued in future generations. To this day the youngest child of the family asks questions about the meaning of the ritual at every Passover. The father retells the familiar story in order to teach the new generation in a way that creates the experience anew rather than simply transmitting information. As Yahweh passed over the houses of Israel's ancestors in Egypt, so every generation will keep the Passover for Yahweh.

12:29-30 Death of the First-born

29At midnight the LORD slew every first-born in the land of Egypt, from the first-born of Pharaoh on the throne to the first-born of the prisoner in the dungeon, as well as all the first-born of the animals. 30Pharaoh arose in the night, he and all his servants and all the Egyptians; and there was loud wailing throughout Egypt, for there was not a house without its dead.

The climactic events in Egypt are a story both of death and new life. They are described with brevity and starkness. There is no lingering over the death of the Egyptians because Israel, like its God, takes no pleasure in such death. It happened in the middle of the night, abruptly and in darkness. The chilling wail dramatizes the horror experienced by every family of Egypt. Like most evil deeds of adults, the death-dealing practice of the Egyptians has its worst impact on the children.

12:31-36 Permission to Depart

31During the night Pharaoh summoned Moses and Aaron and said, "Leave my people at once, you and the Israelites with you! Go and worship the LORD as you said. 32Take your flocks, too, and your herds, as you demanded, and begone; and you will be doing me a favor."
33The Egyptians likewise urged the people on, to hasten their departure from the land; they thought that otherwise they would all die. 34The people, therefore, took their dough before it was leavened, in their kneading bowls wrapped in their cloaks on their shoulders. 35The Israelites did as Moses had commanded: they asked the Egyptians for articles of silver and gold and for clothing. 36The LORD indeed had made the Egyptians so well-disposed toward the people that they let them have whatever they asked for. Thus did they despoil the Egyptians.

With all Pharaoh's resistance gone, he reverses his own order (10:28) and sends for Moses and Aaron. Pharaoh completely surrenders and, along with the Egyptians, hurries the Israelites out of the country. The long-awaited Exodus will be delayed no longer.

The use of unleavened bread reminded the later generations of Israel of their hasty departure from Egypt and the need to always be ready for God's unexpected actions among them. Rather than wait for the bread to rise during the night, the fermenting process was interrupted when the dough had to be disturbed for the sudden departure. The bread would have to be eaten unleavened wherever and whenever they would have their next meal.

As they leave Egypt, the Israelites are the victors. They depart with the silver, gold, and clothing of their captors as if they were the spoils of battle. They do not leave as slaves, but with the clothing and jewelry of a free and victorious people.

12:37-42 Departure from Egypt

[37]The Israelites set out from Rameses for Succoth, about six hundred thousand men on foot, not counting the children. [38]A crowd of mixed ancestry also went up with them, besides their livestock, very numerous flocks and herds. [39]Since the dough they had brought out of Egypt was not leavened, they baked it into unleavened loaves. They had been rushed out of Egypt and had no opportunity even to prepare food for the journey.

[40]The time the Israelites had stayed in Egypt was four hundred and thirty years. [41]At the end of four hundred and thirty years, all the hosts of the LORD left the land of Egypt on this very date. [42]This was a night of vigil for the LORD, as he led them out of the land of Egypt; so on this same night all the Israelites must keep a vigil for the LORD throughout their generations.

The Exodus has begun; an event long anticipated by Israel, repeatedly delayed by Pharaoh, and carefully readied by Yahweh. The historical nature of the event is made concrete by mention of the place of departure and the direction of travel. Yet, the event also transcends its historical specificity through details of its ritual renewal, extending the experience of Exodus to all generations of Israel.

There are many theories attempting to explain the number of people involved in the Exodus. Six hundred thousand men, plus women and children, seems implausibly high. One theory suggests that the word here translated "thousand" originally designated a tribal subsection or clan. Another suggests that the number is hyperbolic, based on the epic nature of the literature. More probably, the number suggests the population of Israel during the time the Yahwist tradition was written, during the reigns of David and Solomon. It thus adds to the timeless understanding that all Israel shares in its foundational experience.

53

The "crowd of mixed ancestry" indicates that others besides the descendants of the twelve sons of Jacob joined in the Exodus. Other oppressed peoples took advantage of the opportunity to experience freedom, and perhaps many of these were joined to the people of Israel not through blood but through belief in their liberating God. Yahweh's redemption is not just for the chosen few, but ultimately for all the world. The call to freedom and life transcends the narrow bounds of race and anticipates the fulfillment of God's promises to make Israel a blessing to all the communities of the earth.

A vigil is a time of careful watching. Since Yahweh had kept the commitment to carefully watch over Israel and bring her to freedom, now Israel is to keep the commitment of Passover through every generation. This night of watching is to be a time of remembering the past and anticipating the future God would bring. The suddenness of Israel's Exodus reminds future generations that Yahweh acts unexpectedly and God's people must always be in vigilant expectation.

12:43-51 Passover Regulations

⁴³The LORD said to Moses and Aaron, "These are the regulations for the Passover. No foreigner may partake of it. ⁴⁴However, any slave who has been bought for money may partake of it, provided you have first circumcised him. ⁴⁵But no transient alien or hired servant may partake of it. ⁴⁶It must be eaten in one and the same house; you may not take any of its flesh outside the house. You shall not break any of its bones. ⁴⁷The whole community of Israel must keep this feast. ⁴⁸If any aliens living among you wish to celebrate the Passover of the LORD, all the males among them must first be circumcised, and then they may join in its observance just like the natives. But no man who is uncircumcised may partake of it. ⁴⁹The law shall be the same for the resident alien as for the native."

⁵⁰All the Israelites did just as the LORD had commanded Moses and Aaron. ⁵¹On that same day the LORD brought the Israelites out of Egypt company by company.

Participation in the Passover feast is a privilege only of those who have been incorporated into the covenant with Yahweh. Foreigners, sojourners, and hired servants could not participate in the feast, though an immigrant or a permanent slave may participate if they enter the covenant by being circumcised. Circumcision became the sign of admission into the community and of participation in the freedom won by Yahweh through the Exodus event.

The regulations for the feast stress the idea of unity in the Passover. It is to be eaten at the same time by the whole community of Israel. The sacrificial lamb is to be roasted whole; none of its bones are to be broken; it is to be eaten in one house. The integrity of the feast creates and expresses unity within the community of Israel.

13:1-16 Consecration of First-born

¹The LORD spoke to Moses and said, ²"Consecrate to me every first-born that opens the womb among the Israelites, both of man and beast, for it belongs to me."

³Moses said to the people, "Remember this day on which you came out of Egypt, that place of slavery. It was with a strong hand that the LORD brought you away. Nothing made with leaven must be eaten. ⁴This day of your departure is in the month of Abib. ⁵Therefore, it is in this month that you must celebrate this rite, after the LORD, your God, has brought you into the land of the Canaanites, Hittites, Amorites, Hivites and Jebusites, which he swore to your fathers he would give you, a land flowing with milk and honey. ⁶For seven days you shall eat unleavened bread, and the seventh day shall also be a festival to the LORD. ⁷Only unleavened bread may be eaten during the seven days; no leaven and nothing leavened may be found in all your territory. ⁸On this day you shall explain to your son, 'This is because of what the LORD did for me when I came out of Egypt.' ⁹It shall be as a sign on your hand and as a reminder on your forehead; thus the law of the LORD will ever be on your lips, because with a strong hand the LORD brought you out of Egypt. ¹⁰Therefore, you shall keep this prescribed rite at its appointed time from year to year.

¹¹"When the LORD, your God, has brought you into the land of the Canaanites, which he swore to you and your fathers he would give you, ¹²you shall dedicate to the LORD every son that opens the womb; and all the male firstlings of your animals shall belong to the LORD. ¹³Every first-born of an ass you shall redeem with a sheep. If you do not redeem it, you shall break its neck. Every first-born son you must redeem. ¹⁴If your son should ask you later on, 'What does this mean?' you shall tell him, 'With a strong hand the LORD brought us out of Egypt, that place of slavery. ¹⁵When Pharaoh stubbornly refused to let us go, the LORD killed every first-born in the land of Egypt, every first-born of man and

of beast. This is why I sacrifice to the LORD everything of the male sex that opens the womb, and why I redeem every first-born of my sons.' [16]Let this, then, be as a sign on your hand and as a pendant on your forehead: with a strong hand the LORD brought us out of Egypt."

Like the Passover meal and the eating of unleavened bread, the consecration of the first-born is intended to ritually commemorate the Exodus event. The death of the Egyptian first-born and the redemption of Israel's first-born on the night of Passover is the foundational event which is renewed in every generation. Since the first-born were saved by Yahweh, they belong to God in a unique way. This redemption was not just an event of the past, but an event to be explained and actualized for each new generation in the land of promise. The children of Israel in every age are to be incorporated into the saving reality of the Exodus.

Like the Passover ritual and the ritual of the unleavened bread, the roots of the consecration of the first-born were more ancient than the Exodus. Sacrifice of the first-born, whether of fruit or animals or persons, was common in surrounding cultures. Yet these ancient rituals were reinterpreted by Israel in light of the Exodus experience. Since human sacrifice was abhorrent to Israel, the first-born were to be consecrated and redeemed with a substitutionary offering just as God redeemed the people of Israel in Egypt. This consecration reminded Israel that the source of all life was the God who redeemed her from slavery and death.

Though the general mandate was to consecrate all first-born to God, including male and female, the historical implementation resulted in specification and exceptions. Only males need to be offered, unclean animals (asses) are to be ransomed with an animal fit for sacrifice (sheep), and sons are to be redeemed with an offering. This law is to be remembered not just with the mind, but integrated into the pattern of one's life. The "sign" on their hands and the "reminder" and "pendant" on their foreheads, while originally metaphorical, came to be physical symbols (tefillin) in later Judaism.

13:17–14:9 Toward the Red Sea

[17]Now, when Pharaoh let the people go, God did not lead them by way of the Philistines' land, though this was the nearest; for he thought, should the people see that they would have to fight,

they might change their minds and return to Egypt. ¹⁸Instead, he rerouted them toward the Red Sea by way of the desert road. In battle array the Israelites marched out of Egypt. ¹⁹Moses also took Joseph's bones along, for Joseph had made the Israelites swear solemnly that, when God should come to them, they would carry his bones away with them.

²⁰Setting out from Succoth, they camped at Etham near the edge of the desert.

²¹The Lord preceded them, in the daytime by means of a column of cloud to show them the way, and at night by means of a column of fire to give them light. Thus they could travel both day and night. ²²Neither the column of cloud by day nor the column of fire by night ever left its place in front of the people.

14 ¹Then the Lord said to Moses, ²"Tell the Israelites to turn about and camp before Pi-hahiroth, between Migdol and the sea. You shall camp in front of Baal-zephon, just opposite, by the sea. ³Pharaoh will then say, 'The Israelites are wandering about aimlessly in the land. The desert has closed in on them.' ⁴Thus will I make Pharaoh so obstinate that he will pursue them. Then I will receive glory through Pharaoh and all his army, and the Egyptians will know that I am the Lord."

This the Israelites did. ⁵When it was reported to the king of Egypt that the people had fled, Pharaoh and his servants changed their minds about them. "What have we done!" they exclaimed. "Why, we have released Israel from our service!" ⁶So Pharaoh made his chariots ready and mustered his soldiers—⁷six hundred first-class chariots and all the other chariots of Egypt, with warriors on them all. ⁸So obstinate had the Lord made Pharaoh that he pursued the Israelites even while they were marching away in triumph. ⁹The Egyptians, then, pursued them; Pharaoh's whole army, his horses, chariots and charioteers, caught up with them as they lay encamped by the sea, at Pi-hahiroth, in front of Baal-zephon.

Though the geographical locations of the Exodus journey are historically uncertain and highly debated, the message of the text is clear. God guided the Israelites and was present with them along the way. The most logical and direct route to the land of promise, along the Mediterranean coast, was not the road taken because Yahweh had a different plan. The seemingly confused and circuitous route of the Israelites both saved them from a disheartening conflict with foreign peoples and prepared for the final defeat of Pharaoh's forces.

There is also uncertainty about the geographical location of the body of water traditionally translated as the "Red Sea." In Hebrew the term is *Yam Suf*: "yam" referring to a sea, lake, or any body of water; "suf" translated as reeds or rushes. The translation "Red Sea" comes from the later Greek translation of the Septuagint version. It was more concerned with the expressing the unlimited implications and creedal aspects of the text than with geographical considerations.

As the climactic event of Israel's liberation begins, reference to the bones of Joseph links the event to the past and the future. The mummification of the body of Joseph closed the Genesis account after Joseph was promised that his body would be brought up from Egypt when Israel was lead out (Gen 50:24-26). It is the final burial of his body in the land of promise that formally closes the book of Joshua after the conquest of the land (Josh 24:32). Thus, the bones of Joseph form a link between Israel's ancestral past in the land of Egypt and the completion of God's promise in the land of Israel.

The guiding and protecting presence of God is represented by a fiery cloud, seen in daylight as a column of cloud and at night as a column of fire (14:24). It is this fiery presence of God which was experienced by Moses at the bush and which will be seen at the great revelation at Mount Sinai. It also describes how later generations continued to experience the presence of God in worship. The Israelites experienced the same guiding and protecting presence of Yahweh when they put incense on the fiery coals of the altar in the Jerusalem temple of later generations (Lev 16:13; 1 Kgs 8:11; Ps 99:7). Cloud and fire are a tangible assurance of God's mysterious presence to the worshipping community in every age.

Two contrasting plans are described: that of Yahweh (13:17–14:4) and that of Pharaoh (14:5-9). The forces of Pharaoh are described in epic terms, and Israel seems to be overwhelmed. Yet, Pharaoh's plan to pursue Israel is part of Yahweh's plan to save Israel in the face of overwhelming odds. As the conflicting plans are set in motion, the stage is set for the final victory of the God of freedom and life over the forces of slavery and death.

14:10-22 Crossing of the Red Sea

[10]Pharaoh was already near when the Israelites looked up and saw that the Egyptians were on the march in pursuit of them. In great fright they cried out to the Lord. [11]And they complained to Moses, "Were there no burial places in Egypt that you had to bring us out here to die in the desert? Why did you do this to us? Why

did you bring us out of Egypt? ¹²Did we not tell you this in Egypt, when we said, 'Leave us alone. Let us serve the Egyptians'? Far better for us to be the slaves of the Egyptians than to die in the desert." ¹³But Moses answered the people, "Fear not! Stand your ground, and you will see the victory the LORD will win for you today. These Egyptians whom you see today you will never see again. ¹⁴The LORD himself will fight for you; you have only to keep still."

¹⁵Then the LORD said to Moses, "Why are you crying out to me? Tell the Israelites to go forward. ¹⁶And you, lift up your staff and, with hand outstretched over the sea, split the sea in two, that the Israelites may pass through it on dry land. ¹⁷But I will make the Egyptians so obstinate that they will go in after them. Then I will receive glory through Pharaoh and all his army, his chariots and charioteers. ¹⁸The Egyptians shall know that I am the LORD, when I receive glory through Pharaoh and his chariots and charioteers."

¹⁹The angel of God, who had been leading Israel's camp, now moved and went around behind them. The column of cloud also, leaving the front, took up its place behind them, ²⁰so that it came between the camp of the Egyptians and that of Israel. But the cloud now became dark, and thus the night passed without the rival camps coming any closer together all night long. ²¹Then Moses stretched out his hand over the sea, and the LORD swept the sea with a strong east wind throughout the night and so turned it into dry land. When the water was thus divided, ²²the Israelites marched into the midst of the sea on dry land, with the water like a wall to their right and to their left.

The grumbling of the people is the first of many murmurings which Israel will voice throughout the wanderings in the wilderness. The reason for their complaint is the very heart of God's saving action on their behalf. The desire to return to the safe security of captivity because of fear of the unknown is a universal response of oppressed people.

Moses is patient with his people this time and responds with words of encouragement and hope. "Fear not" is the encouragement to trust in the power of God being made manifest. The "victory" which Moses assures the people that God will win is the Hebrew word for "salvation." The immediate effect of God's salvation is rescue from the Egyptians, yet it describes more comprehensively the deliverance from oppression experienced by a free people. They are challenged to begin shaping their vision of life according to their experience of freedom rather than the bondage they so painfully remember.

The text shows evidence of at least two separate traditions of this pivotal event. The Yahwist tradition describes God as driving back the waters throughout the night with a strong east wind so that dry land appeared. God's presence then caused the Egyptians to panic, the wheels of their chariots were jammed, and the waters flowed back to their normal depth as the Egyptians were hurled into its midst. In the Priestly tradition, Moses stretches out his hand at God's command and the waters are divided, allowing the Israelites to pass through the sea on dry ground with the waters like a wall to their right and left. As the Egyptians pursue, Moses stretches out his hand again and the returning waters engulf the Egyptian army.

Each tradition expresses a different aspect of the truth about what God had done for Israel. The Yahwist tradition describes the historical event from the point of view of a storyteller. The Priestly tradition looks much more like a liturgical recitation of the event with its careful structure and emphasis on the fulfillment of God's word. Both describe the destruction of the Egyptians and the passage of Israel to freedom through the waters. The final editor retained the integrity of the different traditions and wove them into a single narrative which is greater than the sum of its parts.

14:23–15:21 Destruction of the Egyptians

²³The Egyptians followed in pursuit; all Pharaoh's horses and chariots and charioteers went after them right into the midst of the sea. ²⁴In the night watch just before dawn the LORD cast through the column of the fiery cloud upon the Egyptian force a glance that threw it into a panic; ²⁵and he so clogged their chariot wheels that they could hardly drive. With that the Egyptians sounded the retreat before Israel, because the LORD was fighting for them against the Egyptians.

²⁶Then the LORD told Moses, "Stretch out your hand over the sea, that the water may flow back upon the Egyptians, upon their chariots and their charioteers." ²⁷So Moses stretched out his hand over the sea, and at dawn the sea flowed back to its normal depth. The Egyptians were fleeing head on toward the sea, when the LORD hurled them into its midst. ²⁸As the water flowed back, it covered the chariots and the charioteers of Pharaoh's whole army which had followed the Israelites into the sea. Not a single one of them escaped. ²⁹But the Israelites had marched on dry land through the midst of the sea, with the water like a wall to their right and to

their left. ³⁰Thus the Lord saved Israel on that day from the power of the Egyptians. When Israel saw the Egyptians lying dead on the seashore ³¹and beheld the great power that the Lord had shown against the Egyptians, they feared the Lord and believed in him and in his servant Moses.

15 ¹Then Moses and the Israelites sang this song to the Lord:
I will sing to the Lord, for he is gloriously triumphant;
   horse and chariot he has cast into the sea.
²My strength and my courage is the Lord,
   and he has been my savior.
He is my God, I praise him;
   the God of my father, I extol him.
³The Lord is a warrior,
   Lord is his name!
⁴Pharaoh's chariots and army he hurled into the sea;
   the elite of his officers were submerged in the Red Sea.
⁵The flood waters covered them,
   they sank into the depths like a stone.
⁶Your right hand, O Lord, magnificent in power,
   your right hand, O Lord, has shattered the enemy.
⁷In your great majesty you overthrew your adversaries;
   you loosed your wrath to consume them like stubble.
⁸At a breath of your anger the waters piled up,
   the flowing waters stood like a mound,
   the flood waters congealed in the midst of the sea.
⁹The enemy boasted, "I will pursue and overtake them;
   I will divide the spoils and have my fill of them;
   I will draw my sword; my hand shall despoil them!"
¹⁰When your wind blew, the sea covered them;
   like lead they sank in the mighty waters.
¹¹Who is like to you among the gods, O Lord?
   Who is like to you, magnificent in holiness?
   O terrible in renown, worker of wonders,
¹² when you stretched out your right hand, the earth swallowed
   them!
¹³In your mercy you led the people you redeemed;
   in your strength you guided them to your holy dwelling.
¹⁴The nations heard and quaked;
   anguish gripped the dwellers in Philistia.
¹⁵Then were the princes of Edom dismayed;
   trembling seized the chieftains of Moab;
All the dwellers in Canaan melted away;
¹⁶ terror and dread fell upon them.
By the might of your arm they were frozen like stone,

61

while your people, O LORD, passed over,
while the people you had made your own passed over.
[17]And you brought them in and planted them on the mountain of
your inheritance—
the place where you made your seat, O LORD,
the sanctuary, O LORD, which your hands established.
[18]The LORD shall reign forever and ever.

[19]They sang thus because Pharaoh's horses and chariots and
charioteers had gone into the sea, and the LORD made the waters
of the sea flow back upon them, though the Israelites had marched
on dry land through the midst of the sea. [20]The prophetess Miriam,
Aaron's sister, took a tambourine in her hand, while all the women
went out after her with tambourines, dancing; [21]and she led them
in the refrain:
Sing to the LORD, for he is gloriously triumphant;
horse and chariot he has cast into the sea.

The victory which God accomplished for Israel at the Sea is the primary event of salvation for Israel. Israel's passing through the waters
to freedom and new life is not just a narrative account of what happened that particular night. It represents what God did for Israel
throughout the whole event of Exodus and what God continues to do.
For Israel, the sea symbolizes the forces of destruction, chaos, and death.
The passage through which God led Israel out of the waters, from the
darkness into the dawn, is clearly an image of birthing. God safely leads
Israel through all the powers that rebel against the freedom and life
which Yahweh wills for this newborn people.

The song of chapter 15 brings the saga of Israel's liberation to a
close. It provides a needed break, to express Israel's response to God's
action on their behalf, before moving on to the next phase of Israel's
journey through the wilderness. The song interprets the events that have
happened in cosmic terms, emphasizing their universal effects. It
celebrates not just a single event, but it proclaims the kind of God which
Yahweh is. God continually destroys all those forces opposed to life
and freedom: crushing injustice, overcoming domination, and vanquish-
ing oppression.

The poem is one of the oldest parts of the Hebrew Bible. Its con-
tinuous refrain is praise for Yahweh's magnificent victory at the Sea
(vv. 1, 21). Israel's self-understanding always links her "coming out"
of bondage to her "coming into" the land. The song moves from Yahweh's triumph at the Sea (vv. 1-12) to the conquest of the land where
Yahweh can be worshipped as ruler (vv. 13-18). Having decisively

defeated the king of Egypt, the lord of oppression and death, Yahweh is now worshipped as the God who saved Israel's life and won her freedom.

The joyful ritual led by Miriam was a celebration of God's victory. She initiated a song and dance that would be continued by every generation of Israel. The song is essentially praise, which not only honors Yahweh but gives witness to God throughout the earth.

15:22-27 At Marah and Elim

²²Then Moses led Israel forward from the Red Sea, and they marched out to the desert of Shur. After traveling for three days through the desert without finding water, ²³they arrived at Marah, where they could not drink the water, because it was too bitter. Hence this place was called Marah. ²⁴As the people grumbled against Moses, saying, "What are we to drink?" ²⁵he appealed to the LORD, who pointed out to him a certain piece of wood. When he threw this into the water, the water became fresh.

It was here that the LORD, in making rules and regulations for them, put them to the test. ²⁶"If you really listen to the voice of the LORD, your God," he told them, "and do what is right in his eyes: if you heed his commandments and keep all his precepts, I will not afflict you with any of the diseases with which I afflicted the Egyptians; for I, the LORD, am your healer."

²⁷Then they came to Elim, where there were twelve springs of water and seventy palm trees, and they camped there near the water.

Between Israel's "coming out" of Egypt and her "coming into" the Promised Land was a long journey through the wilderness. Part of this wilderness tradition is found in Israel's journey from the Sea to Mount Sinai (Exod 15–18) and part is found in the journey from Mount Sinai to the borders of the Promised Land (Num 10–36). Throughout this journey in the desert Israel was experiencing the process of being formed into a people. This foundational period of Israel's newborn life was a time marked with testing, failure, and above all, learning to trust in God's constancy in a precarious environment.

In the desert the foundations of Israel's future life take shape. The Israelites' self-identity begins to change as they realize the provider for their life is no longer Pharaoh with his slave wages, but their generous and faithful God. They learn how to exist in freedom, discovering that it requires a sense of responsibility and a whole new attitude toward life. Israel learns what a life of partnership with God implies, what covenanted life requires, the need for solidarity, and the legal and organizational institutions necessitated by that bond.

The route of Israel's journey through the wilderness is uncertain. The various traditions maintained definite place names for each episode; however, those landmarks that were clear to them are no longer clear to us. Many of the stories along the desert route are designed to explain how the place in which the crisis arose got its name.

This first episode in the wilderness narratives sets the pattern for the episodes to follow: a problem arises, the people complain, Moses intercedes with God on behalf of the community, and God generously delivers them. After three days the Israelites had not found water, a necessity for life in the desert. When the water they found was bitter, the people grumbled against Moses. When he turned to Yahweh, Moses was directed to a type of tree which made the water sweet. Moses becomes the mediator of Yahweh's gracious response to Israel's need. Everything that Israel learned about survival in the desert is understood to be the result of the sustaining and guiding providence of the God of life.

This first test of Israel in the wilderness parallels the first plague in Egypt: "they could not drink the water" (7:24; 15:23). We have seen in the plague narratives how disorder and destruction occurs when life is distorted by bondage. When living under the God of life, Israel discovers the abundant potential within life. Human ingenuity and imagination are able to discover the capacity that God has given to life when it is free to flourish.

When Pharaoh hardened his heart, the Egyptians experienced affliction. When Israel opens its heart to listen to God's voice, the people will experience healing and abundant life. Israel is liberated from Pharaoh so that she may have the freedom to serve Yahweh. Obedience to God's commandments and precepts becomes Israel's way of demonstrating her trust in God in the specific situations of life. The call to obedience anticipates God's giving of the law at Mount Sinai, while the grumbling of Israel anticipates the revolt against God and against Moses during the course of the journey. The well-watered abundance of Elim, with its twelve springs, anticipates the land of promise in which Israel will flourish.

istorical info on

16:1-3 The Desert of Sin

¹Having set out from Elim, the whole Israelite community came into the desert of Sin, which is between Elim and Sinai, on the fifteenth day of the second month after their departure from the land of Egypt. ²Here in the desert the whole Israelite community grumbled against Moses and Aaron. ³The Israelites said to them, "Would that we had died at the LORD's hand in the land of Egypt, as we sat by our fleshpots and ate our fill of bread! But you had to lead us into this desert to make the whole community die of famine!"

Just as thirst had led to the Israelites' grumbling at Marah, their hunger prompted their complaining in the Desert of Sin. Presumably after traveling through the desert for a month, they had consumed the provisions with which they had left Egypt. They had not yet learned where to turn for their source of life, so they looked back with longing to the table of Pharaoh. Facing all the uncertainties which freedom creates, the Israelite community regrets their redemption and desires to return to the security of slavery.

16:4-15 The Quail and Manna

⁴Then the LORD said to Moses, "I will now rain down bread from heaven for you. Each day the people are to go out and gather their daily portion; thus will I test them, to see whether they follow my instructions or not. ⁵On the sixth day, however, when they prepare what they bring in, let it be twice as much as they gather on the other days." ⁶So Moses and Aaron told all the Israelites, "At evening you will know that it was the LORD who brought you out of the land of Egypt; ⁷and in the morning you will see the glory of the LORD, as he heeds your grumbling against him. But what are we that you should grumble against us? ⁸When the LORD gives you flesh to eat in the evening," continued Moses, "and in the morning your fill of bread, as he heeds the grumbling you utter against him, what then are we? Your grumbling is not against us, but against the LORD."

⁹Then Moses said to Aaron, "Tell the whole Israelite community: Present yourselves before the LORD, for he has heard your grumbling." ¹⁰When Aaron announced this to the whole Israelite community, they turned toward the desert, and lo, the glory of the LORD appeared in the cloud! ¹¹The LORD spoke to Moses and

said, [12]"I have heard the grumbling of the Israelites. Tell them: In the evening twilight you shall eat flesh, and in the morning you shall have your fill of bread, so that you may know that I, the LORD, am your God."

[13]In the evening quail came up and covered the camp. In the morning a dew lay all about the camp, [14]and when the dew evaporated, there on the surface of the desert were fine flakes like hoarfrost on the ground. [15]On seeing it, the Israelites asked one another, "What is this?" for they did not know what it was. But Moses told them, "This is the bread which the LORD has given you to eat.

Human griping is contrasted with divine generosity. The "grumbling" of the Israelites is mentioned six times in verses 7-12. Remarkably, God does not respond with severity, but the complaints of Israel become the springboard for God's display of grace. Yahweh promises flesh in the evening and bread in the morning so that the people of Israel might know Yahweh as the one who generously sustains their life.

In the seventh plague God rained down hail upon Egypt, destroying the sources of food; now God will "rain down bread from heaven" to provide for the hunger of God's people. In the eighth plague the arrival of the locusts which came and covered the land is described in the same way as the arrival of the quail which covered the camp and provided food. When Israel abides in freedom with God and relies on divine providence, the necessities of life abound.

The ancient authors do not imply that the gifts of manna and quail were inexplicable occurrences. The thin flaky substance which the writer compares with hoarfrost may very well be the secretions of the tamerisk plant or the excretions of the insects which feed on its fruit. Still gathered today by the nomads of the desert, the sugary substance accumulates during the cool of the night and disintegrates in the heat of the day. The quail may be migratory birds that are often exhausted enough to be caught by hand when they land.

The priestly tradition does not emphasize the mere fact of this desert food; the text, rather, accentuates what the people learned about Yahweh from their experience. In the desert they came to realize that God bestows numerous blessings in the context of their daily lives. God's presence is not to be sought after in the extraordinary, in strange and inexplicable events. Rather, divine generosity is discovered in all that contributes to Israel's life. Yahweh is intimately involved in the daily needs of this new community of God's people.

16:16-36 Regulations Regarding the Manna

¹⁶"Now, this is what the Lord has commanded. So gather it that everyone has enough to eat, an omer for each person, as many of you as there are, each man providing for those of his own tent." ¹⁷The Israelites did so. Some gathered a large and some a small amount. ¹⁸But when they measured it out by the omer, he who had gathered a large amount did not have too much, and he who had gathered a small amount did not have too little. They so gathered that everyone had enough to eat. ¹⁹Moses also told them, "Let no one keep any of it over until tomorrow morning." ²⁰But they would not listen to him. When some kept a part of it over until the following morning, it became wormy and rotten. Therefore Moses was displeased with them.

²¹Morning after morning they gathered it, till each had enough to eat; but when the sun grew hot, the manna melted away. ²²On the sixth day they gathered twice as much food, two omers for each person. When all the leaders of the community came and reported this to Moses, ²³he told them, "That is what the Lord prescribed. Tomorrow is a day of complete rest, the sabbath, sacred to the Lord. You may either bake or boil the manna, as you please; but whatever is left put away and keep for the morrow." ²⁴When they put it away for the morrow, as Moses commanded, it did not become rotten or wormy. ²⁵Moses then said, "Eat it today, for today is the sabbath of the Lord. On this day you will not find any of it on the ground. ²⁶On the other six days you can gather it, but on the seventh day, the sabbath, none of it will be there." ²⁷Still, on the seventh day some of the people went out to gather it, although they did not find any. ²⁸Then the Lord said to Moses, "How long will you refuse to keep my commandments and laws? ²⁹Take note! The Lord has given you the sabbath. That is why on the sixth day he gives you food for two days. On the seventh day everyone is to stay home and no one is to go out." ³⁰After that the people rested on the seventh day.

³¹The Israelites called this food manna. It was like coriander seed, but white, and it tasted like wafers made with honey.

³²Moses said, "This is what the Lord has commanded. Keep an omerful of manna for your descendants, that they may see what food I gave you to eat in the desert when I brought you out of the land of Egypt." ³³Moses then told Aaron, "Take an urn and put an omer of manna in it. Then place it before the Lord in safekeeping for your descendants." ³⁴So Aaron placed it in front of the commandments for safekeeping, as the Lord had commanded Moses.

³⁵The Israelites ate this manna for forty years, until they came to settled land; they ate manna until they reached the borders of Canaan. ³⁶[An omer is one tenth of an ephah.]

Yahweh gives Israel the necessities of life. Manna sustains the people with the gift of nourishment; the Sabbath favors Israel with necessary rest and renewal. Yet, with God's gifts, also comes responsibility. The gifts of freedom bring the necessity of discipline. Thus, God tests the Israelites so that God's generosity becomes the occasion for Israel to develop a responsible lifestyle.

The people were to gather only their daily portion of manna. They were to gather it in such a way that everyone had enough to eat and no one had too little. They were not to store the manna or accumulate it for the future; they were to rely on God for the needs of each day.

Setting aside one day each week as special is also a way of living responsibly as a free people. The Sabbath, as a day of solemn rest, expresses the fact that Israel's days of bondage are over. Disengaging from work as a day of hallowed leisure is an opportunity to break from the daily routine of life and an expression of harmony with God's creative design for life. The double portion of manna to be collected on the sixth day insures that daily needs are satisfied while obeying the regulations of the Sabbath.

God's command to preserve a daily provision of manna for posterity will serve as a remembrance of God's care in forming the community of Israel. The enduring memory of the daily "bread from heaven" is to replace their distorted memory of the bread of Egypt (v. 3). The instruction anticipates the command to build the ark of the covenant and the sanctuary in the wilderness to be described later in the text. The jar of manna will be placed in front of the tablets of God's commandments. A sign of God's compassionate care (the manna) and a sign of God's law for Israel (the tablets of the commandments) are to be associated together in Israel's worship.

17:1-7 Water from the Rock

¹From the desert of Sin the whole Israelite community journeyed by stages, as the LORD directed, and encamped at Rephidim.

Here there was no water for the people to drink. ²They quarreled, therefore, with Moses and said, "Give us water to drink." Moses replied, "Why do you quarrel with me? Why do you put the LORD to a test?" ³Here, then, in their thirst for water, the people grumbled against Moses, saying, "Why did you ever make us leave Egypt? Was it just to have us die here of thirst with our children and our livestock?" ⁴So Moses cried out to the LORD, "What shall I do with this people? A little more and they will stone me!" ⁵The LORD answered Moses, "Go over there in front of the people, along with some of the elders of Israel, holding in your hand, as you go, the staff with which you struck the river. ⁶I will be standing there in front of you on the rock in Horeb. Strike the rock, and the water will flow from it for the people to drink." This Moses did, in the presence of the elders of Israel. ⁷The place was called Massah and Meribah, because the Israelites quarreled there and tested the LORD, saying, "Is the LORD in our midst or not?"

The crisis which developed at this stage of the journey is described as the people's "quarrel" with Moses and their "test" of Yahweh. Fearing a rebellion and even his own death by stoning, Moses intercedes with God and once again God graciously sustains the life of Israel. The tradition associated the incident with the place names by which the event was remembered. Massah means a "place of testing" and Meribah means a "place of quarreling."

The people of Israel demonstrate a lack of trust in Yahweh's providential care for them. Testing Yahweh means demanding that God demonstrate concretely and prove to them the divine presence. Verse 7 focuses the issue on the question: "Is the LORD in our midst or not?" The question is incredible in view of God's deliverance of Israel from slavery, God's rescue at the sea, and God's direction and sustenance in the wilderness. As the psalmist sang of Yahweh: "They tested me though they had seen my works" (Ps 95:9).

In this desert land where life is so precarious and death is always threatening, God works through Moses and his staff to provide water for the people. Moses' striking the rock to bring water for the people to drink is the life-giving counterpart to Moses' striking the Nile to make the water unfit to drink in the land of bondage. The tradition of Israel saw much more significance in these events than satisfying physical needs. Yahweh is the Rock upon whom the pilgrim people rely; the flowing water is the life which God constantly provided for them.

17:8-16 Battle with Amalek

⁸At Rephidim, Amalek came and waged war against Israel. ⁹Moses, therefore, said to Joshua, "Pick out certain men, and tomorrow

go out and engage Amalek in battle. I will be standing on top of the hill with the staff of God in my hand." ¹⁰So Joshua did as Moses told him: he engaged Amalek in battle after Moses had climbed to the top of the hill with Aaron and Hur. ¹¹As long as Moses kept his hands raised up, Israel had the better of the fight, but when he let his hands rest, Amalek had the better of the fight. ¹²Moses' hands, however, grew tired; so they put a rock in place for him to sit on. Meanwhile Aaron and Hur supported his hands, one on one side and one on the other, so that his hands remained steady till sunset. ¹³And Joshua mowed down Amalek and his people with the edge of the sword.

¹⁴Then the Lord said to Moses, "Write this down in a document as something to be remembered, and recite it in the ears of Joshua. I will completely blot out the memory of Amalek from under the heavens." ¹⁵Moses also built an altar there, which he called Yahweh-nissi; ¹⁶for he said, "The Lord takes in hand his banner; the Lord will war against Amalek through the centuries."

The Amalekites were a wide-ranging desert tribe who would be enemies of Israel for many generations. The hostilities which began in the wilderness would continue into the land of promise and not end until the time of Israel's monarchy. They attacked at a time of great vulnerability for Israel, seeking to exterminate this newborn people. Like a new Pharaoh in the wilderness, Amalek threatened the freedom and life God had won for Israel. Such threatening powers will continually be a part of Israel's history and Israel's victories over them credited to God.

Again it is Moses who is the instrument of God's victory for Israel. The raised staff of Moses and his devoted presence on top of the hill was a visible expression of Yahweh's presence in the battle. Moses' hands held aloft invited Israel to trust in Yahweh and became an efficacious sign of the power of God at work in saving the life of Israel.

Joshua is first introduced here as Israel's commander in combat. His name means "Yahweh delivers." This battle is the first of many in which Joshua will lead the people of Israel in conquering the land promised to them. His very name indicates that Israel's successes are not determined by her own strength but through human cooperation with God's will.

The altar which commemorated this event was named "Yahweh-nissi" or "The Lord is my standard." The raised standard or banner for Israel was the firm and steady presence of Moses with his hands outstretched. To remember the raised hands of Moses standing as a banner on the hilltop was to recall that the hand of God would be active in Israel's deliverance through the centuries.

18:1-12 Meeting with Jethro

¹Now Moses' father-in-law Jethro, the priest of Midian, heard of all that God had done for Moses and for his people Israel: how the LORD had brought Israel out of Egypt. ²So his father-in-law Jethro took along Zipporah, Moses' wife, whom Moses had sent back to him, ³and her two sons. One of these was called Gershom; for he said, "I am a stranger in a foreign land." ⁴The other was called Eliezer; for he said, "My father's God is my helper; he has rescued me from Pharaoh's sword." ⁵Together with Moses' wife and sons, then, his father-in-law Jethro came to him in the desert where he was encamped near the mountain of God, ⁶and he sent word to Moses, "I, Jethro, your father-in-law, am coming to you, along with your wife and her two sons."

⁷Moses went out to meet his father-in-law, bowed down before him, and kissed him. Having greeted each other, they went into the tent. ⁸Moses then told his father-in-law of all that the LORD had done to Pharaoh and the Egyptians for the sake of Israel, and of all the hardships they had had to endure on their journey, and how the LORD had come to their rescue. ⁹Jethro rejoiced over all the goodness that the LORD had shown Israel in rescuing them from the hands of the Egyptians. ¹⁰"Blessed be the LORD," he said, "who has rescued his people from the hands of Pharaoh and the Egyptians. ¹¹Now I know that the LORD is a deity great beyond any other; for he took occasion of their being dealt with insolently to deliver the people from the power of the Egyptians." ¹²Then Jethro, the father-in-law of Moses, brought a holocaust and other sacrifices to God, and Aaron came with all the elders of Israel to participate with Moses' father-in-law in the meal before God.

In contrast to the hostility of the Amalekites, the Midianites became friends and allies with Israel through the family ties with Moses. The name of Moses' elder son recalls the condition of God's people at his son's birth, "a stranger in a foreign land." The name of his second son expresses the new experience of God's people, "my God is a helper." The text implies that Moses had sent his family back to Midian when conditions grew worse in Egypt. Now that Yahweh has rescued Israel, they are able to be reunited. This moment of reunion becomes an op-

71

portunity to look back and rejoice at what God had accomplished before beginning the momentous events at Mount Sinai.

The focus is on Jethro, Moses' father-in-law, whom Moses greets with deep respect and affection. The experience of Jethro's coming to faith in Yahweh becomes the pattern for entry into the faith community of Israel. First, Moses declares all the mighty acts that God has done for Israel. Having heard the good news proclaimed to him, Jethro rejoices. He then makes his own confession of faith in Yahweh, offers sacrifices, and shares with the people of Israel in a sacred meal.

18:13-27 Appointment of Minor Judges

[13]The next day Moses sat in judgment for the people, who waited about him from morning until evening. [14]When his father-in-law saw all that he was doing for the people, he inquired, "What sort of thing is this that you are doing for the people? Why do you sit alone while all the people have to stand about you from morning till evening?" [15]Moses answered his father-in-law, "The people come to me to consult God. [16]Whenever they have a disagreement, they come to me to have me settle the matter between them and make known to them God's decisions and regulations."

[17]"You are not acting wisely," his father-in-law replied. [18]"You will surely wear yourself out, and not only yourself but also these people with you. The task is too heavy for you; you cannot do it alone. [19]Now, listen to me, and I will give you some advice, that God may be with you. Act as the people's representative before God, bringing to him whatever they have to say. [20]Enlighten them in regard to the decisions and regulations, showing them how they are to live and what they are to do. [21]But you should also look among all the people for able and God-fearing men, trustworthy men who hate dishonest gain, and set them as officers over groups of thousands, of hundreds, of fifties, and of tens. [22]Let these men render decisions for the people in all ordinary cases. More important cases they should refer to you, but all the lesser cases they can settle themselves. Thus, your burden will be lightened, since they will bear it with you. [23]If you do this, when God gives you orders you will be able to stand the strain, and all these people will go home satisfied."

[24]Moses followed the advice of his father-in-law and did all that he had suggested. [25]He picked out able men from all Israel and put them in charge of the people as officers over groups of thousands, of hundreds, of fifties, and of tens. [26]They rendered deci-

sions for the people in all ordinary cases. The more difficult cases they referred to Moses, but all the lesser cases they settled themselves. [27]Then Moses bade farewell to his father-in-law, who went off to his own country.

This text gives some of the oldest indications concerning the formation of Israel's legal traditions. Freedom brought with it the necessity of living responsibly, and a system for promoting justice within the community inevitably developed. The narrative associates Israel's legal system with the covenant to be established at Sinai and makes clear that Yahweh is the source and authority of both the law of Israel and its interpretation in the course of Israel's daily life.

In Israel there was no distinction between divine law and civil law. All of the decisions and regulations that bind Israel as God's people were understood to be related to the covenant which God established with Israel. The covenant was made applicable to the countless problems that inevitably arise in daily existence.

The counsel which Jethro gave Moses is first an affirmation of Moses' role as intermediary between God and the people. Moses is to bring the concerns and problems of Israel before God in order to discern the will of God in their daily life. He is also to be the teacher of Israel, bringing to them an understanding of God's law and clarifying God's expectations.

Second, Jethro's counsel is practical advice about delegation of authority. Moses is counseled to appoint trustworthy officials over various divisions of people to make judgments for them. The more general and less complex disputes would be handled by these judges, while the more difficult problems would be brought to Moses. This arrangement may reflect a later period in Israel's history in which matters for which there was some precedence were handled locally while unique problems which would require a new application of covenant principles would be brought to court in Jerusalem. The narrative makes clear that the developing system of justice always looked back to Moses and the covenant as its original source.

19:1-15 Arrival at Sinai

[1]In the third month after their departure from the land of Egypt, on its first day, the Israelites came to the desert of Sinai. [2]After the journey from Rephidim to the desert of Sinai, they pitched camp.

While Israel was encamped here in front of the mountain, ³Moses went up the mountain to God. Then the LORD called to him and said, "Thus shall you say to the house of Jacob; ⁴tell the Israelites: You have seen for yourselves how I treated the Egyptians and how I bore you up on eagle wings and brought you here to myself. ⁵Therefore, if you hearken to my voice and keep my covenant, you shall be my special possession, dearer to me than all other people, though all the earth is mine. ⁶You shall be to me a kingdom of priests, a holy nation. That is what you must tell the Israelites." ⁷So Moses went and summoned the elders of the people. When he set before them all that the LORD had ordered him to tell them, ⁸the people all answered together, "Everything the LORD has said, we will do." Then Moses brought back to the LORD the response of the people.

⁹The LORD also told him, "I am coming to you in a dense cloud, so that when the people hear me speaking with you, they may always have faith in you also." When Moses, then, had reported to the LORD the response of the people, ¹⁰the LORD added, "Go to the people and have them sanctify themselves today and tomorrow. Make them wash their garments ¹¹and be ready for the third day; for on the third day the LORD will come down on Mount Sinai before the eyes of all the people. ¹²Set limits for the people all around the mountain, and tell them: Take care not to go up the mountain, or even to touch its base. If anyone touches the mountain he must be put to death. ¹³No hand shall touch him; he must be stoned to death or killed with arrows. Such a one, man or beast, must not be allowed to live. Only when the ram's horn resounds may they go up to the mountain." ¹⁴Then Moses came down from the mountain to the people and had them sanctify themselves and wash their garments. ¹⁵He warned them, "Be ready for the third day. Have no intercourse with any woman."

As the people of Israel reach Mount Sinai, the narrative returns to its source. Anticipated since Moses' experience of Yahweh at the burning bush, the movement of Exodus has been to bring Israel to this place of encounter with God. Here God will come to meet Israel and reveal the divine nature more fully, just as God has come to meet Moses to reveal the divine name. Here the people will stay throughout the remainder of the Book of Exodus until the journey continues in Numbers 10:11.

The religious tradition of Israel attached tremendous importance to the covenant-making at Sinai. The covenant which God forms with

Israel here will formally bind them in a relationship which will determine the entire subsequent history of Israel. Unlike their bondage in Egypt under Pharaoh, the covenant with Yahweh will be life-giving and characterized by mutual freedom. Renewed continually throughout history, the covenant became the characteristic feature of Israel's religion.

Verses 3-8 serve as a prologue for all the events that will happen at Sinai and they are a summary of Israel's understanding of covenant. The elevated style and structure of these verses seem to characterize the passage as part of a periodic ceremony of covenant reenactment and renewal. First, there is a proclamation of God's mighty deeds (v. 4); second, the conditions of the covenant are set forth (vv. 5-6); and finally, the people give their free response of commitment (vv. 7-8). This is the pattern which dominated all of Israel's subsequent ceremonies of covenant renewal (Josh 24).

The invitation to covenant is based on God's saving deeds in the past. God is here described as an eagle bearing its young to the mountain. Further developed in Deuteronomy 32:10-11, the image is one of nurture and protection, in which the parent eagle tenderly cares for its young and hovers over them. It is also an image of testing and maturation, in which the eagle helps the young to fly for themselves by catching them as they fall from the nest and bearing them on its outstretched wings. The image is one of gentle encouragement, preferring to elicit a free response from people rather than imposing submission by force.

The conditions for this relationship with God call for Israel to hearken to God's voice and keep God's covenant. It is a personal invitation to experience life more fully, based on the faithfulness that God has already shown in the past. With an affirmative response, the people of Israel would be described by three separate but interrelated images. As God's "special possession" among all other people, Israel would be like the crown jewel of a king's treasure. As a "kingdom of priests" Israel would have special access to Yahweh and would serve as mediators between God and other kingdoms. As a "holy nation" Israel would be set apart from others for the worship and service of God.

Israel's response, "Everything the LORD has said, we will do," indicates the people's enthusiastic acceptance of this relationship with God. It is a pledge to a God to whom they are already closely related. The remaining events at Sinai will unfold the implications of their commitment and reveal more fully the nature of this life-giving God of the covenant.

Moses is instructed to prepare the people for the theophany to come. The text does not specify all that is involved in this sanctification of the people, only that they are to wash their garments and refrain from sexual intercourse. This consecration involves a separation from what is normal and good in daily existence to prepare for an extraordinary encounter with the divine. The mountain too is to be sanctified ground to which no one may approach except Moses. Setting up of ritual boundaries and ritual purification reflects practices later in Israel's history in which people were sealed off from the sacred precincts of the Temple and were prepared for cultic ceremonies.

The "third day," the time of God's manifestation on the mountain, indicates a brief period of time marked by rising anticipation. When the ram's horn sounds, the call both to war and to worship throughout Israel's history, the people may approach the boundary set up by Moses. Yahweh would come in the dense cloud and speak to Moses, thereby affirming him as the mediator of God's word. The many trips of Moses up and down the mountain reinforce his role as mediator of the covenant.

19:16-25 The Great Theophany

¹⁶On the morning of the third day there were peals of thunder and lightning, and a heavy cloud over the mountain, and a very loud trumpet blast, so that all the people in the camp trembled. ¹⁷But Moses led the people out of the camp to meet God, and they stationed themselves at the foot of the mountain. ¹⁸Mount Sinai was all wrapped in smoke, for the LORD came down upon it in fire. The smoke rose from it as though from a furnace, and the whole mountain trembled violently. ¹⁹The trumpet blast grew louder and louder, while Moses was speaking and God answering him with thunder.

²⁰When the LORD came down to the top of Mount Sinai, he summoned Moses to the top of the mountain, and Moses went up to him. ²¹Then the LORD told Moses, "Go down and warn the people not to break through toward the LORD in order to see him; otherwise many of them will be struck down. ²²The priests, too, who approach the LORD must sanctify themselves; else he will vent his anger upon them." ²³Moses said to the LORD, "The people cannot go up to Mount Sinai, for you yourself warned us to set limits around the mountain to make it sacred." ²⁴The LORD repeated, "Go down now! Then come up again along with Aaron. But the priests

and the people must not break through to come up to the LORD; else he will vent his anger upon them." ²⁵So Moses went down to the people and told them this.

The coming of Yahweh begins at daybreak on the third day. In ancient cultures the mountain was the place of divine encounter, a bridge between earth and the heavens. The thunder and lightning, the heavy cloud, the fire and smoke, and the trembling mountain are all biblical expressions for divine power and the manifestation of God's presence. As Moses leads the procession of the people to the mountain, the increasing blast of the ram's horn gives rising intensity to the awesome scene.

It is impossible to distinguish what happened at the historical event and the later reenactment of the event in the covenant renewal. The cultic ceremony as it developed in Israel would have involved a procession to the holy place accompanied by the sounding of trumpets and clouds of incense rising from the sanctuary. For the Hebrew there was only one covenant event in which every ritual renewal shared; thus the passage reflects elements of Israel's worship developed through the centuries.

20:1-17 The Ten Commandments

¹Then God delivered all these commandments:

²"I, the LORD, am your God, who brought you out of the land of Egypt, that place of slavery. ³You shall not have other gods besides me. ⁴You shall not carve idols for yourselves in the shape of anything in the sky above or on the earth below or in the waters beneath the earth; ⁵you shall not bow down before them or worship them. For I, the LORD, your God, am a jealous God, inflicting punishment for their fathers' wickedness on the children of those who hate me, down to the third and fourth generation; ⁶but bestowing mercy down to the thousandth generation, on the children of those who love me and keep my commandments.

⁷"You shall not take the name of the LORD, your God, in vain. For the LORD will not leave unpunished him who takes his name in vain.

⁸"Remember to keep holy the sabbath day. ⁹Six days you may labor and do all your work, ¹⁰but the seventh day is the sabbath of the LORD, your God. No work may be done then either by you, or your son or daughter, or your male or female slave, or your beast, or by the alien who lives with you. ¹¹In six days the LORD

made the heavens and the earth, the sea and all that is in them; but on the seventh day he rested. That is why the LORD has blessed the sabbath day and made it holy.

¹²"Honor your father and your mother, that you may have a long life in the land which the LORD, your God, is giving you.

¹³"You shall not kill.

¹⁴"You shall not commit adultery.

¹⁵"You shall not steal.

¹⁶"You shall not bear false witness against your neighbor.

¹⁷"You shall not covet your neighbor's house. You shall not covet your neighbor's wife, nor his male or female slave, nor his ox or ass, nor anything else that belongs to him."

Though the Decalogue is often taken out of its biblical context for liturgical and catechetical reasons, it is important to see that God's commandments are an integral part of the Sinai narrative. They flow out of the action of God's self-revelation and God's liberating activity among the people of Israel. God's instructions for the life of the community are centered in the self-identification of the living and freeing God. God's commandments, which could have been understood as another form of bondage for Israel, are understood as the gracious instruction of the God who leads them through obedience to greater freedom and fuller life.

Since the Sinai narrative is all about the unique interpersonal relationship which God established with Israel, the law is understood to be a gift of God's generosity and an opportunity for Israel to personally respond to what God has done on her behalf. For every generation, responding to God's commandments, just as worshipping God in liturgy, would be a way of sharing in the redeeming actions of the Exodus and living in the covenant.

The experience of Egypt had shown how the subversion of God's will had created bondage, oppression, and death. The law of Israel is given so that the experience of Egypt will not be repeated among them. Thus, the Ten Commandments flow from Yahweh "who brought you out of Egypt, that place of slavery." When the law is obeyed in love, it promotes and enhances the quality of life which God desires for the people of Israel and it guarantees that they will continue to live in freedom.

The list of Ten Commandments (literally, "ten words," 34:28; Deut 4:13; 10:4) originally consisted of ten brief imperatives. Their collection in this simple, easy-to-remember form kept them alive in the community through the ages. In time these brief words were expanded as the general principles were applied in new ways to respond to particular needs.

These commandments were not at all comprehensive. They were the foundation and starting point for the ongoing task of ethical reflection among the newborn people. Yet, the privileged status of these ten among all the laws of Israel is emphasized by the narrative. These are the words spoken by Yahweh in the hearing of all the people as they gathered around the sacred mountain. They are laws dealing with the most important principles and boundaries which would define life within covenant and community.

Though the tradition that the commandments are ten in number is strong, various communities have arranged the numbering differently through the centuries. The sequence of commandments varies within Jewish tradition and the ten commandments are never isolated from the larger body of biblical law in the rabbinical writings. The Catholic tradition generally treats verses 3-6 as a single commandment and Deuteronomy 5:21 as two precepts. The Reformed tradition treats verses 4-6 as the second commandment and considers verse 17 (Deut 5:21) as the tenth commandment.

The first commandment enjoins Israel to an exclusive relationship with Yahweh. The command does not indicate that Israel's earliest belief was monotheism—the understanding that there is only one God for the whole world. Israel, however, was to live in absolute and singular loyalty to Yahweh, thus rejecting a relationship with all other gods.

The prohibition against creating idols was originally intended to forbid the creation of any images of Yahweh for Israel's worship. The purpose was to protect Israel's understanding of Yahweh as the God who exists in total freedom. God's self-revelation was through the divine word acting in Israel's history. They were to worship Yahweh without compromising the transcendent yet personal divine presence by an image that could be contained and confined. The imageless cult of Israel set her off from all the other surrounding cultures. God's presence and power could not be controlled by the use of images or any other technique of worship. Israel always used verbal images of God because they have the capacity to express God's relatedness in ways that static images do not.

The prohibition was later expanded to include images of foreign gods. The challenge of Canaanite religion constantly tempted Israel to pervert religion into an activity for obtaining blessings from God. Yahweh is described as "jealous," a metaphor from the sphere of marriage. Unfaithfulness to the commitment with God is contagious for the next generations and thus evokes the righteous anger of God for several generations. In contrast, commitment to the covenant evokes unlimited goodness generation after generation.

The prohibition against using the name of God for empty and useless purposes was to protect the sacredness of the divine name. God's name, either the revealed name "Yahweh" or any of the divine titles by which Israel called upon God, was to be invoked, honored, and praised. The divine name expressed the very nature of God which Israel was privileged to have continually revealed to her. Abuse of the divine name was seen to be so serious that the commandment was expanded later in history to contain a solemn warning for disobedience.

The "Sabbath" was a day of "stopping," a day of cessation from the normal daily routine. For Israel this day was to be made "holy," set aside for something special, as a day belonging to Yahweh. This is the most expanded of all the commandments, with clauses added through the centuries to justify and apply this central tenet of Israel's life. The priestly tradition added the justification in verse 11 connecting the Sabbath with God's creation. Yet the pattern of the seven days in the creation account of Genesis 1 is patterned on the fact that Israel already kept this seventh day as a day of rest. The priestly writer thus ties the Sabbath observance with God's rhythmical plan for all of life. Israelites, slaves, animals, and foreigners are all to cease from labor on the Sabbath.

An earlier tradition associated the Sabbath with Israel's experience of liberation. While in slavery there was no interruption of the unending round of forced labor. Moses' request for time to worship God in the desert was met with scorn by Pharaoh. The Sabbath became a remembrance for Israel of her former slavery and God's deliverance (Deut 5:15). Thus, the Sabbath was understood by Israel as a divine gift related directly to the God who created life and the God who gave Israel freedom.

To "honor" one's parents was to have a respect and reverence that is usually reserved for God. Honor for God is the foundation of the covenant; honor for fathers and mothers is the foundation of all other human relationships. The commandment refers to the reverence and care adults are to have toward their elderly parents and to the respectful obedience children are to offer their mother and father. God is the giver of all life, so parents together are the channel of that life to their children. The promise of long life and prosperity associated with the commandment assures that one's own life is enhanced by honoring the bearers of that life.

Since human life is such a sacred gift, to kill a life is forbidden. The negative imperative forbids acts of death-dealing violence that arise out of vengeance, malice, anger, or desire for personal gain. Though usually intended to describe intentional killing, or murder, the verb is also used to describe unintentional killing. Since God is the giver and lord of life, Israel developed many laws designed to insure that human life was protected within the covenant community.

The command against adultery is intended to protect the sanctity of the marriage bond and refers to either the man or the woman as the subject. The offense is a crime not only against the human relationship, but it effects the covenant with God in a serious way. Faithfulness to the marital relationship reflected faithfulness to the covenant with Yahweh. Like the worship of other gods, adultery was a turning away from commitment to Yahweh. The severe penalty of death attached to adultery in Israel's legal tradition indicates the seriousness of the rupture it creates.

The prohibition against stealing is the third in a series of commands that consist of two Hebrew words: a negative particle and a four letter verb form without a definite object. Many think that these simple negative imperatives were the original form of many of the commandments. The prohibition indicates that Israel understood theft of a person's property as a violation against the person. Those in covenant with Yahweh are not to steal because disruption of relationships within community also disrupt one's relationship with God.

The root of the command against false witness was Israel's legal process. The communal institution of justice depended on truthfulness. Yet, the testimony one gives before the elders in a legal proceeding is not something separate from the witness one gives in all the other circumstances of communal life. The term "neighbor" refers to a fellow member of the covenant community. The prohibition was understood to refer to any lie which harms the reputation of a neighbor, whether it be slanderous or deceptive talk or damaging rumor about another. Not only individuals but the well-being of community is damaged by a lack of trustworthiness among its members.

The final commandment refers to a subjective attitude whereas the previous prohibitions were directed against an objective action. The

81

verb translated "covet" means to desire obsessively or lust after for one-self. "Neighbor's house" includes everything connected with the full-ness of life of one who is in covenant community: one's entire family and one's entire property. The command was expanded to specify what covetousness meant in the context of covenant community. Deu-teronomy 5:21 detached "wife" into a separate commandment for un-known reasons.

The subjective attitude of covetousness often leads to objective mis-use of what is not one's own. It is an attitude of discontent which leads to violation of the other commandments. It thus serves as a summary warning because of its comprehensiveness and its reference to the in-terior disposition that can lead to social disorder.

The Ten Commandments not only place boundaries on the com-munity of Israel, but also encourage the development of the covenant. The law expresses Israel's commitment to be faithful to the Exodus ex-perience. Though the precepts are formulated negatively, they implicitly commend their positive side. For example, not abusing God's name invites praise of God, not killing implies efforts to respect life, not com-mitting adultery encourages faithful relationships in marriage, and not bearing false witness suggests honoring the good name of others. Is-rael recognized that the integrity of the covenant demanded mutual re-spect for persons—for their life, their relationships, their reputation, and their belongings.

20:18-26 The Fear of God

¹⁸When the people witnessed the thunder and lightning, the trum-pet blast and the mountain smoking, they all feared and trembled. So they took up a position much farther away ¹⁹and said to Moses, "You speak to us, and we will listen; but let not God speak to us, or we shall die." ²⁰Moses answered the people, "Do not be afraid, for God has come to you only to test you and put his fear upon you, lest you should sin." ²¹Still the people remained at a distance, while Moses approached the cloud where God was.

²²The LORD told Moses, "Thus shall you speak to the Israelites: You have seen for yourselves that I have spoken to you from heaven. ²³Do not make anything to rank with me; neither gods of silver nor gods of gold shall you make for yourselves.

²⁴"An altar of earth you shall make for me, and upon it you shall sacrifice your holocausts and peace offerings, your sheep and your oxen. In whatever place I choose for the remembrance of my

name I will come to you and bless you. ²⁵If you make an altar of
stone for me, do not build it of cut stone, for by putting a tool
to it you desecrate it. ²⁶You shall not go up by steps to my altar,
on which you must not be indecently uncovered.

Overwhelmed by the astonishing and dreadful experience of the divine presence, the people withdrew in trembling fear. The role of Moses
as intermediary between God and the people is then confirmed by Israel. Previously, Moses had been set apart and made mediator of the
covenant by God's choice. Now, the people affirm his role by request-
ing that he take their place before the divine presence and then report
to them the words of Yahweh.

His intercessory role continues throughout the Exodus tradition as
Moses becomes the suffering mediator of his people. He not only speaks
for God to Israel, but he represents Israel before God. As mediator he
will receive the additional laws that follow (20:23f.), seal the covenant
with Yahweh (24:1f.), plead for Israel at the golden calf episode (32:1f.),
and finally, die outside the Promised Land because of the sin of the
people (Deut 1:37).

The divine self-manifestation amidst awesome spectacle is not
designed to impose a trembling fear, but to evoke a reverential fear
within the people. God's purpose, "to put his fear upon you, lest you
should sin," is to establish the personal attitude necessary to obey the
divine law. With such a respect for their relationship with Yahweh,
the people would be able to hold these principles of life as the focal
priority of their lives.

Verse 22 begins a long collection of laws, continuing through 23:33,
called the "book of the covenant" (24:7). The verse serves to link the
complex of laws to the experience at Sinai. Though Moses communicates the law to Israel, the covenant regulations clearly have their origin in Yahweh. Obedience to the law, then, is not a matter of outward
adherence to an impersonal theory of justice, but a response to a personal God who has entered into a relationship with Israel and calls them
to order all of their communal life under this covenant.

The first law defines the essence of Israel's faithfulness: exclusive
worship of Yahweh alone. This loyalty to Yahweh is the foundation
of all the other regulations which are multiple expressions of that singular reality. The instructions concerning the altar continue this concern for proper worship. It stipulates that altars of sacrifice are to be
made from the earth. When they are made from stone, they are not

to be cut with tools. No explicit reasons are given for these specifications, though they are probably designed to distinguish Israel's worship from that of surrounding cultures. Altars are to be constructed at those places chosen by divine initiative; therefore, multiple sanctuaries are allowed throughout the land, but only at places of legitimate worship.

At these sanctuaries, God promises to come and bless the worshippers. Israel's cult is to be seen as the setting in which God's presence can be experienced with certainty and focused intensity. Israel can be loyal to God only because God assures divine loyalty to them. It is this context of worship and blessings that provides the setting for Israel's life of obedience to God. The God who gives commandments to be obeyed is also the God who makes promises.

21:1-11 Laws Regarding Slaves

[1]"These are the rules you shall lay before them. [2]When you purchase a Hebrew slave, he is to serve you for six years, but in the seventh year he shall be given his freedom without cost. [3]If he comes into service alone, he shall leave alone; if he comes with a wife, his wife shall leave with him. [4]But if his master gives him a wife and she bears him sons or daughters, the woman and her children shall remain the master's property and the man shall leave alone. [5]If, however, the slave declares, 'I am devoted to my master and my wife and children; I will not go free,' [6]his master shall bring him to God and there, at the door or doorpost, he shall pierce his ear with an awl, thus keeping him as his slave forever.

[7]"When a man sells his daughter as a slave, she shall not go free as male slaves do. [8]But if her master, who had destined her for himself, dislikes her, he shall let her be redeemed. He has no right to sell her to a foreigner, since he has broken faith with her. [9]If he destines her for his son, he shall treat her like a daughter. [10]If he takes another wife, he shall not withhold her food, her clothing, or her conjugal rights. [11]If he does not grant her these three things, she shall be given her freedom absolutely, without cost to her.

The designation given for the laws that follow is "rules" or "ordinances." These are best understood as guiding decisions or precedent cases that draw out the implications of the Ten Commandments in the practical order. These judgments apply the generally stated principles to the specific issues that need attention within a particular time and context.

In responding justly to specific situations, God's compassionate care for Israel becomes the paradigm for Israel's treatment of others. As God cared for the oppressed, showing them how to live in freedom, so Israel is to show compassion for others. God will continue to hear the cries of the oppressed as Israel continues to enter into the suffering of those in need.

Slavery was an accepted institution within the society of Israel. The ordinances concern the treatment of slaves, giving guidance for the care of both male (vv. 2-6) and female (vv. 7-11) slaves. Hope for freedom was to live in the heart of those held in servitude. The major stipulation of the law was that a slave was to be released in the seventh year. This is followed by several "if" clauses which introduce particular refinements of the law. One may become a permanent slave under his own volition because of devotion to his family and his owner.

The law is different for female slaves, since they were to become the wife or concubine of their owners. They were not to be released in the seventh year (though this seems to be changed later in Deut 15:12). The owner may take her for himself, give her to his son as a wife, or let her be redeemed by her family. The conditions for each case specify certain rights of female slaves and protection from inhumane treatment. If any of these rights are violated, she is to be given her freedom.

21:12-32 Personal Injury

¹²"Whoever strikes a man a mortal blow must be put to death. ¹³He, however, who did not hunt a man down, but caused his death by an act of God, may flee to a place which I will set apart for this purpose. ¹⁴But when a man kills another after maliciously scheming to do so, you must take him even from my altar and put him to death. ¹⁵Whoever strikes his father or mother shall be put to death.

¹⁶"A kidnaper, whether he sells his victim or still has him when caught, shall be put to death.

¹⁷"Whoever curses his father or mother shall be put to death.

¹⁸"When men quarrel and one strikes the other with a stone or with his fist, not mortally, but enough to put him in bed, ¹⁹the one who struck the blow shall be acquitted, provided the other can get up and walk around with the help of his staff. Still, he

must compensate him for his enforced idleness and provide for his complete cure.

²⁰"When a man strikes his male or female slave with a rod so hard that the slave dies under his hand, he shall be punished. ²¹If, however, the slave survives for a day or two, he is not to be punished, since the slave is his own property.

²²"When men have a fight and hurt a pregnant woman, so that she suffers a miscarriage, but no further injury, the guilty one shall be fined as much as the woman's husband demands of him, and he shall pay in the presence of the judges. ²³But if injury ensues, you shall give life for life, ²⁴eye for eye, tooth for tooth, hand for hand, foot for foot, ²⁵burn for burn, wound for wound, stripe for stripe.

²⁶"When a man strikes his male or female slave in the eye and destroys the use of the eye, he shall let the slave go free in compensation for the eye. ²⁷If he knocks out a tooth of his male or female slave, he shall let the slave go free in compensation for the tooth.

²⁸"When an ox gores a man or a woman to death, the ox must be stoned; its flesh may not be eaten. The owner of the ox, however, shall go unpunished. ²⁹But if an ox was previously in the habit of goring people and its owner, though warned, would not keep it in; should it then kill a man or a woman, not only must the ox be stoned, but its owner also must be put to death. ³⁰If, however, a fine is imposed on him, he must pay in ransom for his life whatever amount is imposed on him. ³¹This law applies if it is a boy or a girl that the ox gores. ³²But if it is a male or a female slave that it gores, he must pay the owner of the slave thirty shekels of silver, and the ox must be stoned.

This series of rules deals with those inflicting harm on others. Situations calling for the death penalty are listed first (vv. 12-17) followed by those calling for lesser penalties. The penalty of death is to be imposed for these offenses: murder, stealing another person for sale into slavery, and striking or cursing one's parent.

Verse 13 makes a distinction between murder and accidental death. If a fatal blow to another is not preplanned, the perpetrator may go to a place of sanctuary from the death penalty. Though the place of sanctuary is not specified, the reference to God's altar in verse 14 seems to indicate that the place of safety was any altar of Yahweh.

Actions inflicting less serious damage on the community are more numerous. The general principle guiding such personal injuries is the law of retaliation (vv. 23-25). The legal principle guards against unbridled revenge by insisting on proportionate compensation for injuries. It also provides greater equality before the law for those of lower social status. The wealthy were not allowed to merely pay a fine for injury done.

Slaves, however, do not qualify for equal compensation for harm done to them. Yet, the concern for slaves in the law is remarkably humanitarian for the ancient world. If a master injures a slave, whether with the loss of an eye or a tooth, the slave is to be freed. When a slave is mistreated, the slave becomes an oppressed person and therefore ought to be liberated.

21:33–22:5 Property Damage

³³"When a man uncovers or digs a cistern and does not cover it over again, should an ox or an ass fall into it, ³⁴the owner of the cistern must make good by restoring the value of the animal to its owner; the dead animal, however, he may keep.

³⁵"When one man's ox hurts another's ox so badly that it dies, they shall sell the live ox and divide this money as well as the dead animal equally between them. ³⁶But if it was known that the ox was previously in the habit of goring and its owner would not keep it in, he must make full restitution, an ox for an ox; but the dead animal he may keep.

³⁷"When a man steals an ox or a sheep and slaughters or sells it, he shall restore five oxen for the one ox, and four sheep for the one sheep.

22 ¹"[If a thief is caught in the act of housebreaking and beaten to death, there is no bloodguilt involved. ²But if after sunrise he is thus beaten, there is bloodguilt.] He must make full restitution. If he has nothing, he shall be sold to pay for his theft. ³If what he stole is found alive in his possession, be it an ox, an ass or a sheep, he shall restore two animals for each one stolen.

⁴"When a man is burning over a field or a vineyard, if he lets the fire spread so that it burns in another's field, he must make restitution with the best produce of his own field or vineyard. ⁵If the fire spreads further, and catches on to thorn bushes, so that shocked grain or standing grain or the field itself is burned up, the one who started the fire must make full restitution.

These laws deal with damage to property resulting from negligence, theft, and fire. The general principle for these crimes against property is proper restitution. The payment in money or kind to be given to the one wronged is often greater than the damage caused. In the case of theft of an ox or sheep, the thief is to pay fivefold for an ox and fourfold for a sheep. A thief who cannot make restitution is to be sold into slavery to pay for his theft.

22:6-14 Trusts and Loans

6"When a man gives money or any article to another for safekeeping and it is stolen from the latter's house, the thief, if caught, must make two-fold restitution. 7If the thief is not caught, the owner of the house shall be brought to God, to swear that he himself did not lay hands on his neighbor's property. 8In every question of dishonest appropriation, whether it be about an ox, or an ass, or a sheep, or a garment, or anything else that has disappeared, where another claims that the thing is his, both parties shall present their case before God; the one whom God convicts must make two-fold restitution to the other.

9"When a man gives an ass, or an ox, or a sheep, or any other animal to another for safekeeping, if it dies, or is maimed or snatched away, without anyone witnessing the fact, 10the custodian shall swear by the Lord that he did not lay hands on his neighbor's property; the owner must accept the oath, and no restitution is to be made. 11But if the custodian is really guilty of theft, he must make restitution to the owner. 12If it has been killed by a wild beast, let him bring it as evidence, and he need not make restitution for the mangled animal.

13"When a man borrows an animal from his neighbor, if it is maimed or dies while the owner is not present, the man must make restitution. 14But if the owner is present, he need not make restitution. If it was hired, this was covered by the price of its hire.

These rules deal with various cases involving loss or theft of property put in the care of another. Those to whom property is entrusted must be aware of their own liability. When something of value is missing when an owner comes to claim it, a thief must be sought. If one is found, the case is simply resolved by requiring a double compensation from the thief. If a thief is not found, the one who accepted the trust must be brought into the presence of God so that his innocence or culpability may be established.

The judicial process is closely linked to the religious aspects of Israel's life. Verses 7, 8 and 10 indicate that God enters into the process and attends personally to matters of justice. The decision is rendered in the sanctuary, either by a divine oracle or by a judge who has authority to speak divine judgments. The process also involves an oath before God with the understanding that Yahweh as witness to the oath was its guarantor.

22:15–23:9 Social Laws

¹⁵"When a man seduces a virgin who is not betrothed, and lies with her, he shall pay her marriage price and marry her. ¹⁶If her father refuses to give her to him, he must still pay him the customary marriage price for virgins.

¹⁷"You shall not let a sorceress live.

¹⁸"Anyone who lies with an animal shall be put to death.

¹⁹"Whoever sacrifices to any god, except to the LORD alone, shall be doomed.

²⁰"You shall not molest or oppress an alien, for you were once aliens yourselves in the land of Egypt. ²¹You shall not wrong any widow or orphan. ²²If ever you wrong them and they cry out to me, I will surely hear their cry. ²³My wrath will flare up, and I will kill you with the sword; then your own wives will be widows, and your children orphans.

²⁴"If you lend money to one of your poor neighbors among my people, you shall not act like an extortioner toward him by demanding interest from him. ²⁵If you take your neighbor's cloak as a pledge, you shall return it to him before sunset; ²⁶for this cloak of his is the only covering he has for his body. What else has he to sleep in? If he cries out to me, I will hear him; for I am compassionate.

²⁷"You shall not revile God, nor curse a prince of your people.

²⁸"You shall not delay the offering of your harvest and your press. You shall give me the first-born of your sons. ²⁹You must do the same with your oxen and your sheep; for seven days the firstling may stay with its mother, but on the eighth day you must give it to me.

³⁰"You shall be men sacred to me. Flesh torn to pieces in the field you shall not eat; throw it to the dogs.

23 ¹"You shall not repeat a false report. Do not join the wicked in putting your hand, as an unjust witness, upon anyone. ²Neither shall you allege the example of the many as an excuse for doing wrong, nor shall you, when testifying in a lawsuit, side with the many in perverting justice. ³You shall not favor a poor man in his lawsuit.

⁴"When you come upon your enemy's ox or ass going astray, see to it that it is returned to him. ⁵When you notice the ass of one who hates you lying prostrate under its burden, by no means desert him; help him, rather, to raise it up.

⁶"You shall not deny one of your needy fellow men his rights in his lawsuit. ⁷You shall keep away from anything dishonest. The innocent and the just you shall not put to death, nor shall you acquit the guilty. ⁸Never take a bribe, for a bribe blinds even the most clear-sighted and twists the words even of the just. ⁹You shall not oppress an alien; you well know how it feels to be an alien, since you were once aliens yourselves in the land of Egypt.

Sexual promiscuity is condemned in Israel because it fails to protect the exploited person from the social consequences. The seduction of an unengaged maiden impaired her chances for a respectable marriage by taking away her virginity. Thus, the man is required to take full responsibility for his action by paying the customary marriage price and by marrying the girl. If the father of the girl opposes the marriage, the seducer is still to pay a sum equivalent to the marriage price.

The laws beginning with verse 17 return to the apodictic form: "You (whoever) shall (not) . . . ." Modern attempts to separate religious, social, and personal ethics do not hold for Israel's laws. Verses 17-19 deal with three offenses calling for the death penalty. The sorceress was identified with pagan practice because she sought to interpret and control the future, thus escaping or altering the will and work of Yahweh. Copulation with an animal is condemned because of its association with fertility worship among the surrounding cultures. Sacrificing to another god is a violation against the First Commandment, and like the other two offenses, is a direct affront to Yahweh.

Verses 20-26 reflect an intense concern for the disadvantaged and weakest members of society. Resident aliens, those living in a community other than their own, are classified with widows and orphans as needing special protection. Without security and family support and without a husband and father, they were vulnerable to abuse and exploitation. Mistreatment of the defenseless members of society calls forth the wrath of Yahweh. The reverse side of God's compassion is the severe divine judgment for those who are victimizers.

If the poor are forced to borrow money, the one who advances money is not to charge interest. If collateral is held by the creditor, it is to be returned before it causes hardship. The cloak taken by the creditor is to be returned before sundown because it serves as the bedding for the impoverished one. The poor are to be treated, thus, as fellow members of the covenant family of God.

These commands are accompanied by exhortation. The motivation for obedience is found by repeated reference to the experience of Exodus (22:20; 23:9). When the people of Israel mistreat the disadvantaged, they violate their own history and disavow those saving acts of liberation which made them who they are. Those who received the gift of freedom and life must continue to extend those gifts to others.

The principle of avoiding injustice and listening to the cries of the oppressed is an invitation to extend these laws to ever new situations. Changing historical and social circumstances challenge Israel to constantly revise these particular rules and apply the principles in new ways. Ongoing discernment of God's will continued to adapt these guiding decisions for the society of Israel as new occasions taught new responsibilities.

Verses 27-30 may be classified as holiness laws, which set Israel apart as sacred to Yahweh. They were not to show any disrespect for Yahweh. Thus, they were not to curse a leader of the covenant community for such an act would be contempt for the divine authority given him. Another act of disrespect for Yahweh would be to hold back that to which God is entitled, whether from the fields, the vineyards, the womb, the herd or flock. An appropriate act of thanksgiving to God is the joyous and generous offering of the first fruits, the first-born sons and the first-born animals.

The first verses of chapter 23 give admonitions concerning Israel's judicial system. Those involved in a trial are not to give false testimony or spread rumors that would prejudice the case; they are not to follow the majority view to the detriment of justice; nor are they to accept a bribe. They are to acquit the innocent and condemn the guilty, being careful not to give an unfair advantage to the poor yet giving the needy and the alien their full rights (Lev 19:15).

Verses 4-5 challenge the people of Israel to realize that justice, such as the return of lost goods and offering assistance to one in need, is due even to one's personal enemies. Obedience to the covenant means refusal to take advantage of another's misfortune because he happens to be an enemy. Permitting evil to happen to another is contrary to the new perspective one is to have toward all people in need.

23:10-19 Religious Laws

¹⁰"For six years you may sow your land and gather in its produce. ¹¹But the seventh year you shall let the land lie untilled and unharvested, that the poor among you may eat of it and the beasts of the field may eat what the poor leave. So also shall you do in regard to your vineyard and your olive grove.

¹²"For six days you may do your work, but on the seventh day you must rest, that your ox and your ass may also have rest, and that the son of your maidservant and the alien may be refreshed. ¹³Give heed to all that I have told you.

"Never mention the name of any other god; it shall not be heard from your lips.

¹⁴"Three times a year you shall celebrate a pilgrim feast to me. ¹⁵You shall keep the feast of Unleavened Bread. As I have commanded you, you must eat unleavened bread for seven days at the prescribed time in the month of Abib, for it was then that you came out of Egypt. No one shall appear before me empty-handed. ¹⁶You shall also keep the feast of the grain harvest with the first of the crop that you have sown in the field; and finally, the feast at the fruit harvest at the end of the year, when you gather in the produce from the fields. ¹⁷Thrice a year shall all your men appear before the Lord God.

¹⁸"You shall not offer the blood of my sacrifice with leavened bread; nor shall the fat of my feast be kept overnight till the next day. ¹⁹The choicest first fruits of your soil you shall bring to the house of the Lord, your God.

"You shall not boil a kid in its mother's milk.

The pattern of the Sabbath year is the same as that of the Sabbath day. In the year of rest, after six years of sowing and harvesting, the land is to be left alone. This applies to the cultivation of grain fields as well as the pruning and harvesting of the vineyards and olive orchards. Though the original motivation for this year is uncertain, it receives various explanations throughout the Hebrew Scriptures. In Exodus the motivation of social concern comes to the fore. Whatever the land produces without cultivation, the poor of the land are to have, and whatever they leave, the animals are to have.

Likewise, the seventh day is motivated by concern for the refreshment of all, including the poor, the alien, and the animals. Worship of God and ritual concerns are not separated from wider human concerns and issues of justice.

Verse 13 forms a summary statement urging obedience to all the rules that have been stated. It also reinforces Israel's central command prohibiting worship of any deity except Yahweh alone. The presence of God in every sphere of life is emphasized by all the ordinances that have preceded and by the three pilgrim feasts that mark key moments in the yearly agricultural cycle of Israel's existence.

The feast of Unleavened Bread, in the spring, marked the time of the first harvest, the barley harvest planted in the winter. The feast is here associated with the yearly commemoration of the Exodus. Pilgrimage to the shrine included an offering of some of the first grain in thanksgiving to Yahweh. The feast of the grain harvest marked the harvest of the wheat crop seven weeks later. Later tradition called this the feast of Weeks (or Sevens) or Pentecost, because it occurred on the fiftieth day. Jewish tradition associated the feast with the giving of the Law. The feast of the fruit harvest was the largest festival of thanksgiving, occurring in autumn as the final ingathering. It was later called the feast of Booths (or Tabernacles or Tents), commemorating Israel's time of nomadic wandering in the wilderness.

Other miscellaneous instructions relate to Israel's ritual. Leaven was seen as an impurity and was unfit for use in sacrifice. The fat of the sacrificial animal, like the blood, was to be offered to God and burned entirely. Boiling a kid in its mother's milk was a Canaanite practice that was seen as abhorrent by Israel.

23:20-33 Reward of Fidelity

²⁰"See, I am sending an angel before you, to guard you on the way and bring you to the place I have prepared. ²¹Be attentive to him and heed his voice. Do not rebel against him, for he will not forgive your sin. My authority resides in him. ²²If you heed his voice and carry out all I tell you, I will be an enemy to your enemies and a foe to your foes.

²³"My angel will go before you and bring you to the Amorites, Hittites, Perizzites, Canaanites, Hivites and Jebusites; and I will wipe them out. ²⁴Therefore, you shall not bow down in worship before their gods, nor shall you make anything like them; rather, you must demolish them and smash their sacred pillars. ²⁵The Lord, your God, you shall worship; then I will bless your food and drink, and I will remove all sickness from your midst; ²⁶no woman in your land will be barren or miscarry; and I will give you a full span of life.

[27]"I will have the fear of me precede you, so that I will throw into panic every nation you reach. I will make all your enemies turn from you in flight, [28]and ahead of you I will send hornets to drive the Hivites, Canaanites and Hittites out of your way. [29]But not in one year will I drive them all out before you; else the land will become so desolate that the wild beasts will multiply against you. [30]Instead, I will drive them out little by little before you, until you have grown numerous enough to take possession of the land. [31]I will set your boundaries from the Red Sea to the sea of the Philistines, and from the desert to the River; all who dwell in this land I will hand over to you to be driven out of your way. [32]You shall not make a covenant with them or their gods. [33]They must not abide in your land, lest they make you sin against me by ensnaring you into worshiping their gods."

God assures Israel of the blessings of the divine presence on their journey to the Promised Land. "Angel," as in 3:2 and 14:19, is any form under which God's guiding and protecting presence is experienced by Israel. God's blessings are manifested in those things that provide abundant life for Israel: deliverance from enemies (vv. 22-24), nourishment and health (v. 25), fertility and long life (v. 26), and secure possession of the land (v. 27).

The land to be entered and settled by Israel is anticipated in this section: its conquest, its blessings, its magnitude, and its purity from the worship of other gods. Though Yahweh promised that Israel would inherit the land, it would be a gradual possession. The extent of the land is an idealized projection that was never historically realized. The sea of the Philistines is the Mediterranean Sea; the river is the Euphrates.

The Book of the Covenant ends as it began, with the command for exclusive devotion to Yahweh. All that lies between are the many and varied ways of expressing that devotion in the life of Israel. The first commandment is the binding theme that makes such a diverse collection of ordinances a singular code.

24:1-11 Ratification of the Covenant

[1]Moses himself was told, "Come up to the Lord, you and Aaron, with Nadab, Abihu, and seventy of the elders of Israel. You shall all worship at some distance, [2]but Moses alone is to come close to the Lord; the others shall not come too near, and the people shall not come up at all with Moses."

³When Moses came to the people and related all the words and ordinances of the Lord, they all answered with one voice, "We will do everything that the Lord has told us." ⁴Moses then wrote down all the words of the Lord and, rising early the next day, he erected at the foot of the mountain an altar and twelve pillars for the twelve tribes of Israel. ⁵Then, having sent certain young men of the Israelites to offer holocausts and sacrifice young bulls as peace offerings to the Lord, ⁶Moses took half of the blood and put it in large bowls; the other half he splashed on the altar. ⁷Taking the book of the covenant, he read it aloud to the people, who answered, "All that the Lord has said, we will heed and do." ⁸Then he took the blood and sprinkled it on the people, saying, "This is the blood of the covenant which the Lord has made with you in accordance with all these words of his."

⁹Moses then went up with Aaron, Nadab, Abihu, and seventy elders of Israel, ¹⁰and they beheld the God of Israel. Under his feet there appeared to be sapphire tilework, as clear as the sky itself. ¹¹Yet he did not smite these chosen Israelites. After gazing on God, they could still eat and drink.

This chapter concludes the narrative of Sinai which began in chapter 19. The teaching conveyed through God's revelation to Moses is now shared with the people. Israel responds faithfully and a solemn covenant relationship is ratified with appropriate ritual. Israel's leaders are then given further authorization for their ongoing role by receiving an intimate experience of Yahweh's presence as they eat the covenant meal.

A threefold gradation is made: Moses alone, the chosen mediator between God and Israel, is to come close to God on the mountain; Aaron, two of his sons, and seventy elders of Israel are to accompany Moses up the mountain but remain at a distance; and the people are not to climb up the mountain at all. The purpose of the leaders' approach is to worship Yahweh. Though verses 1-2 fit better with verses 9-11, the final editor has sandwiched verses 3-8. The covenant ritual with all the people was placed within the context of God's manifested presence to those leaders chosen to enact and interpret God's revelation.

Moses reported all the "words" and "ordinances" of Yahweh, the Ten Commandments along with the guiding principles of the law. After the people committed themselves to God by their freely acclaimed assent, Moses wrote down all the words to define the legal terms of the covenant agreement. He then set up the altar and twelve pillars to represent the relationship being established between each of the tribes and Yahweh.

The sacrifices offered were of two kinds: the "holocausts," the offerings that were completely burned on the altar, and "peace offerings," the fat of which was burned and the rest shared among the participants as a communion. The blood of the sacrifice both symbolized and contained life (Lev 17:14). Pouring the blood on the altar was the sign that Yahweh was the Lord of life. When Moses then proclaimed from the Book of the Covenant, he was proclaiming the words of the God of life. The people's commitment joined them with this God who was the source of their new life. The sprinkling of the sacrificial blood on the people established a community of life between Yahweh and Israel. The "blood of the covenant" (v. 8) is the seal and pledge of this relationship. The people of Israel are now called to the task of living the quality of life which the covenant entails.

The intimate contact of Israel's leaders with their God (v. 9f.) prepares them for their service of teaching and judging. The vision of God on the mountain is awe-inspiring and full of mystery beyond the power of words to express. The rich sapphire pavement at God's feet suggests the blueness of the heavens. The sight of the pavement may indicate that they were prostrate before God and did not lift their faces, since no one could do so and live (33:20). The divine effulgence indicated a real and personal presence of God with Moses and the leaders of the people as they celebrated the communion meal. The sacrificial banquet on the mountain implied a real sharing of life between Yahweh and Israel.

24:12-18 Moses on the Mountain

¹²The Lord said to Moses, "Come up to me on the mountain and, while you are there, I will give you the stone tablets on which I have written the commandments intended for their instruction." ¹³So Moses set out with Joshua, his aide, and went up to the mountain of God. ¹⁴The elders, however, had been told by him, "Wait here for us until we return to you. Aaron and Hur are staying with you. If anyone has a complaint, let him refer the matter to them." ¹⁵After Moses had gone up, a cloud covered the mountain. ¹⁶The glory of the Lord settled upon Mount Sinai. The cloud covered it for six days, and on the seventh day he called to Moses from the midst of the cloud. ¹⁷To the Israelites the glory of the Lord was seen as a consuming fire on the mountaintop. ¹⁸But Moses

passed into the midst of the cloud as he went up on the mountain; and there he stayed for forty days and forty nights.

This scene provides the context for the next large section of material—the instructions for the divine Dwelling (chapters 25-31). God's command for Moses to ascend the mountain and receive the stone tablets will be concluded in 31:18 as God gives the two tablets which Moses then brings down the mountain in 32:15. The mention of Joshua as Moses' attendant anticipates his subsequent role in chapter 32. Aaron and Hur are asked to wait below along with the elders to deal with any problems that might arise. Their charge sets the stage for the disaster to follow in chapter 32.

The Priestly tradition provides the material which begins in verse 15 and continues throughout the instructions for the divine Dwelling. The "glory of Yahweh," the visible manifestation of God, is priestly language. This glory is shown in the descending cloud and the consuming fire seen by the people on the mountaintop. This appearance of God in cloud and fire will characterize God's presence in the Dwelling at the end of Exodus (40:38). What happened at Sinai will be continued in the Dwelling.

25:1-9 Collection of Materials

¹This is what the LORD then said to Moses: ²"Tell the Israelites to take up a collection for me. From every man you shall accept the contribution that his heart prompts him to give me. ³These are the contributions you shall accept from them: gold, silver and bronze; ⁴violet, purple and scarlet yarn; fine linen and goat hair; ⁵rams' skins dyed red, and tahash skins; acacia wood; ⁶oil for the light; spices for the anointing oil and for the fragrant incense; ⁷onyx stones and other gems for mounting on the ephod and the breastpiece.

⁸"They shall make a sanctuary for me, that I may dwell in their midst. ⁹This Dwelling and all its furnishings you shall make exactly according to the pattern that I will now show you.

The people of Israel have moved from servitude to Pharaoh to service of Yahweh. Both Israel's servitude and service were expressed in building: the supply cities in Egypt at the beginning of Exodus and the Dwelling for God as the book moves to its conclusion. The first building project was commanded under forced slavery; the Dwelling is built willingly in freedom.

Chapters 25–31 are instructions for building Israel's sanctuary; chapters 35–40 describe the construction of the sanctuary. Such a volume of material focused on the instructions for Israel's tabernacle indicates the importance of worship for the life of the people of Israel. This book of Israel's origins describes Israel's two basic institutions, the law and the sanctuary. Both form Israel's new existence in freedom, giving that life an ethical shape and a liturgical shape.

The final editors of Exodus intend these chapters to be understood within the context of God's further revelation to Moses on the mountain. Now that Israel had entered into covenant, God could reveal the means for continually expressing and experiencing that covenant in worship. Moses is called still further up the mountain to receive instructions for the elements of Israel's ongoing worship as God's people.

The call for material is prefaced by the instruction that all contributions are to be made freely—not compelled—as each one's heart is prompted to give. The materials themselves are some of the finest and rarest available. The metals are listed in descending value, as are the colored yarns made from rare dyes extracted from shellfish and insects.

The purpose of the sanctuary is stated by Yahweh: "that I may dwell in their midst." Israel's God will leave the remote mountain, the particular abode for the gods of the ancient Near East, to dwell in the center of human community. The people may have confidence that God dwells there in the midst of the insecurities of the wilderness. The question of God's people at Massah and Meribah, "Is the LORD in our midst or not?" is answered with the assurance that the divine presence can be found in a tangible place which moves along the journey with Israel.

25:10-22 Plan of the Ark

¹⁰"You shall make an ark of acacia wood, two and a half cubits long, one and a half cubits wide, and one and a half cubits high. ¹¹Plate it inside and outside with pure gold, and put a molding of gold around the top of it. ¹²Cast four gold rings and fasten them on the four supports of the ark, two rings on one side and two on the opposite side. ¹³Then make poles of acacia wood and plate them with gold. ¹⁴These poles you are to put through the rings on the sides of the ark, for carrying it; ¹⁵they must remain in the rings of the ark and never be withdrawn. ¹⁶In the ark you are to put the commandments which I will give you.

¹⁷"You shall then make a propitiatory of pure gold, two cubits and a half long, and one and a half cubits wide. ¹⁸Make two cheru-

bim of beaten gold for the two ends of the propitiatory, [19]fastening them so that one cherub springs direct from each end. [20]The cherubim shall have their wings spread out above, covering the propitiatory with them; they shall be turned toward each other, but with their faces looking toward the propitiatory. [21]This propitiatory you shall then place on top of the ark. In the ark itself you are to put the commandments which I will give you. [22]There I will meet you and there, from above the propitiatory, between the two cherubim on the ark of the commandments, I will tell you all the commands that I wish you to give the Israelites.

The ark takes first place among the elements of the Dwelling due to its central importance in the whole structure. It is the symbol and vehicle of God's nearness with Israel, serving as both container for the symbols of the covenant and as throne for Yahweh's presence. Its size was unimposing; a cubit represented the distance from one's elbow to fingertips. The opulence of its gold plating and molding suggests its importance as the most sacred object in the Dwelling.

The golden rings and poles emphasize both the mobile character of the ark and its untouchable holiness. The carrying poles are to remain inserted in the rings at all times. The ark is to be carried with the people as they are on the move. It is a reminder of the ongoing journey of God's people and stands over against any attempts to confine God in an immovable abode.

The covering for the ark, made of gold, is the same dimensions as the ark. The cherubim were creatures with human heads but having wings and the body of an animal. They were commonly placed as guardians of thrones and temples in Mesopotamia. According to the priestly understanding, it was above the ark cover and between the cherubim that Yahweh's presence was most powerfully experienced. There Moses would meet God and receive the divine instructions for the people of Israel.

25:23-30 The Table

[23]"You shall also make a table of acacia wood, two cubits long, a cubit wide, and a cubit and a half high. [24]Plate it with pure gold and make a molding of gold around it. [25]Surround it with a frame, a handbreadth high, with a molding of gold around the frame. [26]You shall also make four rings of gold for it and fasten them at the four corners, one at each leg, [27]on two opposite sides of the

frame as holders for the poles to carry the table. ²⁸These poles for carrying the table you shall make of acacia wood and plate with gold. ²⁹Of pure gold you shall make its plates and cups, as well as its pitchers and bowls for pouring libations. ³⁰On the table you shall always keep showbread set before me.

The table, made from the same material as the ark, was also to be transported with poles. Upon it was to be kept loaves of bread, best translated as "bread of God's presence." Leviticus 24:5-9 describes how the bread and wine were to be placed in the golden vessels. The twelve loaves, to be replaced each Sabbath, were a sacred offering made to Yahweh as a pledge of the covenant. The bread offering was accompanied by libations of wine and burning incense on the table. Such a lavish display indicates that the table was a symbol of God's sustaining and nourishing presence with Israel.

25:31-40 The Lampstand

³¹"You shall make a lampstand of pure beaten gold—its shaft and branches—with its cups and knobs and petals springing directly from it. ³²Six branches are to extend from the sides of the lampstand, three branches on one side, and three on the other. ³³On one branch there are to be three cups, shaped like almond blossoms, each with its knob and petals; on the opposite branch there are to be three cups, shaped like almond blossoms, each with its knobs and petals; and so for the six branches that extend from the lampstand. ³⁴On the shaft there are to be four cups, shaped like almond blossoms, with their knobs and petals, ³⁵including a knob below each of the three pairs of branches that extend from the lampstand. ³⁶Their knobs and branches shall so spring from it that the whole will form but a single piece of pure beaten gold. ³⁷You shall then make seven lamps for it and so set up the lamps that they shed their light on the space in front of the lampstand. ³⁸These, as well as the trimming shears and trays, must be of pure gold. ³⁹Use a talent of pure gold for the lampstand and all its appurtenances. ⁴⁰See that you make them according to the pattern shown you on the mountain.

The lampstand (menorah), made of hammered gold, was to suggest an almond tree. Its main shaft had three branches growing out of each side. The shaft and six branches were each capped with an open flower design. This same golden blossom was repeated four times along the length of the shaft and three times along each branch. The lamp-stand would hold seven oil lamps at the end of the shaft and each branch.

Functionally, the lampstand was to provide light for the Dwelling. Symbolically, its organic pattern suggested the fertility and life which God provides and the lamps suggested the continual presence of Yahweh made known through the constant fire in their midst.

26:1-14 The Tent Cloth

¹"The Dwelling itself you shall make out of sheets woven of fine linen twined and of violet, purple and scarlet yarn, with cherubim embroidered on them. ²The length of each shall be twenty-eight cubits, and the width four cubits; all the sheets shall be of the same size. ³Five of the sheets are to be sewed together, edge to edge; and the same for the other five. ⁴Make loops of violet yarn along the edge of the end sheet in one set, and the same along the edge of the end sheet in the other set. ⁵There are to be fifty loops along the edge of the end sheet in the first set, and fifty loops along the edge of the corresponding sheet in the second set, and so placed that the loops are directly opposite each other. ⁶Then make fifty clasps of gold, with which to join the two sets of sheets, so that the Dwelling forms one whole.

⁷"Also make sheets woven of goat hair, to be used as a tent covering over the Dwelling. ⁸Eleven such sheets are to be made; the length of each shall be thirty cubits, and the width four cubits: all eleven sheets shall be of the same size. ⁹Sew five of the sheets, edge to edge, into one set, and the other six sheets into another set. Use the sixth sheet double at the front of the tent. ¹⁰Make fifty loops along the edge of the end sheet in one set, and fifty loops along the edge of the end sheet in the second set. ¹¹Also make fifty bronze clasps and put them into the loops, to join the tent into one whole. ¹²There will be an extra half sheet of tent covering, which shall be allowed to hang down over the rear of the Dwelling. ¹³Likewise, the sheets of the tent will have an extra cubit's length to be left hanging down on either side of the Dwelling to protect it. ¹⁴Over the tent itself you shall make a covering of rams' skins dyed red, and above that, a covering of tahash skins.

The people of Israel certainly must have had some type of moving tent representing Yahweh's presence among them in their Exodus journey. The meeting tent in which Moses communicated with God (33:7f.)

is perhaps the earliest form of this more elaborate Dwelling revealed through Moses on Sinai. Yet, how much of the present material is historical and how much is a product of Israel's later construction of sanctuaries and temples is open for speculation.

The Dwelling itself is an elaborate, but portable shrine. Many elements of the structure seem unrealistic for a people traveling through the desert. The Dwelling strongly reflects elements of the later Temple of Solomon. It may also reflect earlier elements of the tabernacle at Shiloh (Joshua 18:1) and the tent that David built for the ark (2 Sam 6:17). It is both a historical sanctuary and a paradigmatic model for all of Israel's temples.

The Dwelling is described not as a temporary institution, but one that will continue through all generations. All the people of Israel continue to experience through time both the law and the sanctuary revealed on Sinai. Just as the law has a foundational form but includes variations and adaptations throughout history, so the basic structure of Israel's worship has a foundation with modifications and adjustments made throughout history.

Since the Priestly tradition was edited during the time of the Exile, the writers are looking back through the days of the glorious temple of Solomon to the desert sanctuary, and they are looking forward to the future rebuilding of the Temple after their Exile. Through reading the text, a majestic sanctuary is summoned in the mind through memory of the past and hope for the future. The sanctuary thus evoked unites the people of Israel in every age with their worshipping ancestors throughout history.

The network of tapestries that comprise the inner part of the structure are made of fine linen and dyed yarns and the two halves are held together with fifty golden clasps. Cherubim are embroidered on the linen sheets which could be seen from inside the structure. Over this inner lining were placed sheets made of goat hair which hung a cubit longer on each side to cover the tapestry. Finally, two outer coverings of animal skins protected the structure from the elements.

26:15-30 The Wooden Walls

¹⁵"You shall make boards of acacia wood as walls for the Dwelling. ¹⁶The length of each board is to be ten cubits, and its width one and a half cubits. ¹⁷Each board shall have two arms that shall serve to fasten the boards in line. In this way all the boards of the

Dwelling are to be made. [18]Set up the boards of the Dwelling as follows: twenty boards on the south side, [19]with forty silver pedestals under the twenty boards, so that there are two pedestals under each board, at its two arms; [20]twenty boards on the other side of the Dwelling, the north side, [21]with their forty silver pedestals, two under each board; [22]six boards for the rear of the Dwelling, to the west; [23]and two boards for the corners at the rear of the Dwelling. [24]These two shall be double at the bottom, and likewise double at the top, to the first ring. That is how both boards in the corners are to be made. [25]Thus, there shall be in the rear eight boards, with their sixteen silver pedestals, two pedestals under each board. [26]Also make bars of acacia wood: five for the boards on one side of the Dwelling, [27]five for those on the other side, and five for those at the rear, toward the west. [28]The center bar, at the middle of the boards, shall reach across from end to end. [29]Plate the boards with gold, and make gold rings on them as holders for the bars, which are also to be plated with gold. [30]You shall erect the Dwelling according to the pattern shown you on the mountain.

The cloth was supported by a series of upright frames made of acacia wood set into silver pedestals. The supports were strengthened by cross-bars to be held in place by gold rings attached to the upright frames. The frame formed a rectangular structure, with upright supports on three sides, with two specially constructed corner supports, and open to the east.

Though described in some detail, there are many uncertainties about the construction. Our understanding of Hebrew technical terms like "boards," "arms," "pedestals," and "bars" is incomplete. The structure is designed to facilitate portability, so that the entire structure could be transported and reassembled in a short period of time.

26:31-37 The Veils

[31]"You shall have a veil woven of violet, purple and scarlet yarn, and of fine linen twined, with cherubim embroidered on it. [32]It is to be hung on four gold-plated columns of acacia wood, which shall have hooks of gold and shall rest on four silver pedestals. [33]Hang the veil from clasps. The ark of the commandments you shall bring inside, behind this veil which divides the holy place from the holy of holies. [34]Set the propitiatory on the ark of the commandments in the holy of holies.

³⁵"Outside the veil you shall place the table and the lampstand, the latter on the south side of the Dwelling, opposite the table, which is to be put on the north side. ³⁶For the entrance of the tent make a variegated curtain of violet, purple and scarlet yarn and of fine linen twined. ³⁷Make five columns of acacia wood for this curtain; have them plated with gold, with their hooks of gold; and cast five bronze pedestals for them.

A veil made of fine linen and embroidered with cherubim divided the Dwelling into two sections: the most holy place, the "holy of holies," and the larger holy place. The ark of the covenant was to be placed behind the veil in the "holy of holies." The table and the lampstand were to be placed outside the veil, opposite each other in the holy place. The open east end of the Dwelling was to be closed by a curtain, made of the same material as the inner veil but embroidered in multicolored patterns.

27:1-8 The Altar of Holocaust

¹"You shall make an altar of acacia wood, on a square, five cubits long and five cubits wide; it shall be three cubits high. ²At the four corners there are to be horns, so made that they spring directly from the altar. You shall then plate it with bronze. ³Make pots for removing the ashes, as well as shovels, basins, forks and fire pans, all of which shall be of bronze. ⁴Make a grating of bronze network for it; this is to have four bronze rings, one at each of its four corners. ⁵Put it down around the altar, on the ground. This network is to be half as high as the altar. ⁶You shall also make poles of acacia wood for the altar, and plate them with bronze. ⁷These poles are to be put through the rings, so that they are on either side of the altar when it is carried. ⁸Make the altar itself in the form of a hollow box, just as it was shown you on the mountain.

An altar for offering animal sacrifices was to be made of acacia and overlaid with bronze. The altar was to have horn-like projections at each of its four corners. Various utensils for the sacrifices were also to be made of bronze. A grate was to be used presumably to hold the fire and the offering while allowing the ashes and grease to fall below. The whole construction was to be hollow for easier transport.

27:9-19 Court of the Dwelling

⁹"You shall also make a court for the Dwelling. On the south side the court shall have hangings a hundred cubits long, woven of fine linen twined, ¹⁰with twenty columns and twenty pedestals of bronze; the hooks and bands on the columns shall be of silver. ¹¹On the north side there shall be similar hangings, a hundred cubits long, with twenty columns and twenty pedestals of bronze; the hooks and bands on the columns shall be of silver. ¹²On the west side, across the width of the court, there shall be hangings, fifty cubits long, with ten columns and ten pedestals. ¹³The width of the court on the east side shall be fifty cubits. ¹⁴On one side there shall be hangings to the extent of fifteen cubits, with three columns and three pedestals; ¹⁵on the other side there shall be hangings to the extent of fifteen cubits, with three columns and three pedestals.

¹⁶"At the entrance of the court there shall be a variegated curtain, twenty cubits long, woven of violet, purple and scarlet yarn and of fine linen twined. It shall have four columns and four pedestals.

¹⁷"All the columns around the court shall have bands and hooks of silver, and pedestals of bronze. ¹⁸The enclosure of the court is to be one hundred cubits long, fifty cubits wide, and five cubits high. Fine linen twined must be used, and the pedestals must be of bronze. ¹⁹All the fittings of the Dwelling, whatever be their use, as well as all its tent pegs and all the tent pegs of the court, must be of bronze.

The courtyard was to surround the sanctuary and separate the activities of worship from the world outside. The court was enclosed by hangings of fine linen stretched between a series of sixty columns set in bronze pedestals. The entrance on the east was to be covered with a screen made of the same material and pattern as the screen covering the entrance to the holy place. The court was considered as part of the Dwelling, the area where public ceremonies took place.

27:20-21 Oil for the Lamps

²⁰"You shall order the Israelites to bring you clear oil of crushed olives, to be used for the light, so that you may keep lamps burning regularly. ²¹From evening to morning Aaron and his sons shall maintain them before the LORD in the meeting tent, outside the veil which hangs in front of the commandments. This shall be a perpetual ordinance for the Israelites throughout their generations.

105

The oil used in the lampstand was to be provided by the people of Israel and tended by the priests. It was to be the purest form of olive oil, extracted by hand rather than pressed, as is fitting for the place of its use. Such oil gives a bright, clean light with little smoke. The lamps are always to be kept burning throughout the night in front of the holy of holies from generation to generation.

28:1-5 The Priestly Vestments

¹"From among the Israelites have your brother Aaron, together with his sons Nadab, Abihu, Eleazar and Ithamar, brought to you, that they may be my priests. ²For the glorious adornment of your brother Aaron you shall have sacred vestments made. ³Therefore, to the various expert workmen whom I have endowed with skill, you shall give instructions to make such vestments for Aaron as will set him apart for his sacred service as my priest. ⁴These are the vestments they shall make: a breastpiece, an ephod, a robe, a brocaded tunic, a miter and a sash. In making these sacred vestments which your brother Aaron and his sons are to wear in serving as my priests, ⁵they shall use gold, violet, purple and scarlet yarn and fine linen.

With the description of the Dwelling complete, the text now turns to the priesthood of Israel who will minister within it. The priesthood became a hereditary office with priests tracing their ancestry to Aaron. As mediators between Yahweh and Israel, the priests presented sacrifices to God, made legal decisions about God's will, pronounced blessings upon the people, and tended to the sacred services within the Dwelling.

The wardrobe described here represents an evolution of design as the vestments developed through the centuries. It is probable that some of the elaborate vestments described here were originally worn by the kings of Israel as they performed their sacred duties as Yahweh's anointed ones. They were later adapted for priestly use, especially after the demise of the monarchy during the time of the Exile.

The focus of the text is on the vestments of Aaron, the high priest. They are to be made for "glorious adornment" by artists specially endowed by Yahweh. Made from the same splendid materials as the sanctuary, the vestments matched the grandeur of the place in which the priest ministered and they set the priest apart for sacred service.

28:6-30 The Ephod and Breastpiece

⁶"The ephod they shall make of gold thread and of violet, purple and scarlet yarn, embroidered on cloth of fine linen twined. ⁷It shall have a pair of shoulder straps joined to its two upper ends. ⁸The embroidered belt on the ephod shall extend out from it and, like it, be made of gold thread, of violet, purple and scarlet yarn, and of fine linen twined.

⁹"Get two onyx stones and engrave on them the names of the sons of Israel: ¹⁰six of their names on one stone, and the other six on the other stone, in the order of their birth. ¹¹As a gem-cutter engraves a seal, so shall you have the two stones engraved with the names of the sons of Israel and then mounted in gold filigree work. ¹²Set these two stones on the shoulder straps of the ephod as memorial stones of the sons of Israel. Thus Aaron shall bear their names on his shoulders as a reminder before the Lord. ¹³Make filigree rosettes of gold, ¹⁴as well as two chains of pure gold, twisted like cords, and fasten the cordlike chains to the filigree rosettes.

¹⁵"The breastpiece of decision you shall also have made, embroidered like the ephod with gold thread and violet, purple and scarlet yarn on cloth of fine linen twined. ¹⁶It is to be square when folded double, a span high and a span wide. ¹⁷On it you shall mount four rows of precious stones: in the first row, a carnelian, a topaz and an emerald; ¹⁸in the second row, a garnet, a sapphire and a beryl; ¹⁹in the third row, a jacinth, an agate and an amethyst; ²⁰in the fourth row, a chrysolite, an onyx and a jasper. These stones are to be mounted in gold filigree work, ²¹twelve of them to match the names of the sons of Israel, each stone engraved like a seal with the name of one of the twelve tribes.

²²"When the chains of pure gold, twisted like cords, have been made for the breastpiece, ²³you shall then make two rings of gold for it and fasten them to the two upper ends of the breastpiece. ²⁴The gold cords are then to be fastened to the two rings at the upper ends of the breastpiece, ²⁵the other two ends of the cords being fastened in front to the two filigree rosettes which are attached to the shoulder straps of the ephod. ²⁶Make two other rings of gold and put them on the two lower ends of the breastpiece, on its edge that faces the ephod. ²⁷Then make two more rings of gold and fasten them to the bottom of the shoulder straps next to where they join the ephod in front, just above its embroidered belt. ²⁸Violet ribbons shall bind the rings of the breastpiece to the rings of the ephod, so that the breastpiece will stay right above the embroidered belt of the ephod and not swing loose from it.

²⁹"Whenever Aaron enters the sanctuary, he will thus bear the names of the sons of Israel on the breastpiece of decision over his heart as a constant reminder before the LORD. ³⁰In this breastpiece of decision you shall put the Urim and Thummim, that they may be over Aaron's heart whenever he enters the presence of the LORD. Thus he shall always bear the decisions for the Israelites over his heart in the LORD's presence.

Ephod is the Hebrew word for a garment, the function of which is not fully known. It seems to be a kind of apron or vest with a decorated belt around the waist. The shoulderpieces are designed to hold up the garment and to provide the setting for the two engraved onyx stones. Bearing the names of the twelve sons of Israel, these stones served as symbolic reminders that the priest represented all the people of Israel in the presence of God.

The "breastpiece of decision" was a square pouch, a handspan in length and width, woven with the same material as the ephod. On it were mounted four rows of three gemstones each, engraved with the names of the twelve tribes of Israel. A system of golden rings and gold and violet cords attached the breastpiece firmly to the shoulderpieces and the ephod so that it would lie close to the chest.

The Urim and Thummim were an oracular device kept within the breastpiece and used by the high priest for interpreting the decisions of Yahweh. How the message of Yahweh was made known through them is uncertain (1 Sam 14:41). Verses 29-39 three times repeat the phrases "over Aaron's/his heart" and "in the presence of Yahweh." Aaron holds the people of Israel close to his heart when he enters the sanctuary to worship or to discern the decisions of Yahweh for them.

28:31-43 Other Vestments

³¹"The robe of the ephod you shall make entirely of violet material. ³²It shall have an opening for the head in the center, and around this opening there shall be a selvage, woven as at the opening of a shirt, to keep it from being torn. ³³All around the hem at the bottom you shall make pomegranates, woven of violet, purple and scarlet yarn and fine linen twined, with gold bells between them; ³⁴first a gold bell, then a pomegranate, and thus alternating all around the hem of the robe. ³⁵Aaron shall wear it when minister-

ing, that its tinkling may be heard as he enters and leaves the LORD's presence in the sanctuary; else he will die.

³⁶"You shall also make a plate of pure gold and engrave on it, as on a seal engraving, "Sacred to the LORD." ³⁷This plate is to be tied over the miter with a violet ribbon in such a way that it rests on the front of the miter, ³⁸over Aaron's forehead. Since Aaron bears whatever guilt the Israelites may incur in consecrating any of their sacred gifts, this plate must always be over his forehead, so that they may find favor with the LORD.

³⁹"The tunic of fine linen shall be brocaded. The miter shall be made of fine linen. The sash shall be of variegated work.

⁴⁰"Likewise, for the glorious adornment of Aaron's sons you shall have tunics and sashes and turbans made. ⁴¹With these you shall clothe your brother Aaron and his sons. Anoint and ordain them, consecrating them as my priests. ⁴²You must also make linen drawers for them, to cover their naked flesh from their loins to their thighs. ⁴³Aaron and his sons shall wear them whenever they go into the meeting tent or approach the altar to minister in the sanctuary, lest they incur guilt and die. This shall be a perpetual ordinance for him and for his descendants.

Under the ephod and breastpiece the high priest was to wear a violet robe. This was a sleeveless garment made of one piece with an opening for slipping it on over the head. Alternating around the bottom of the robe were pomegranates and golden bells. Pomegranates were common symbols of fertility and life. The bells could be heard tinkling as an announcement of entry into Yahweh's presence. They would be heard by the people outside during the sacred ceremonies so that they would know the priest is still alive before the awesome divine presence.

The engraved plate, to be placed on the front of the miter, signified that the high priest was set apart for God's service. It further indicated that all Israel, whom Aaron represented in God's presence, was sacred to Yahweh. Though the high priest bore the guilt of Israel upon himself, the plate symbolized that God continues to redeem the chosen people.

The tunic was a long shirt-like garment worn under the robe. The sash was wrapped around the tunic at the waist. The miter was a ceremonial headgear made of linen wrapped around the head. The vestments of the other priests were simpler, consisting of tunics, sashes, and less elaborate caps. The linen undergarments were to fulfill the rule of 20:26. Vesting in sacred garments was part of the first stage in the ritual of consecration for Israel's priesthood.

29:1-9 Consecration of the Priests

¹"This is the rite you shall perform in consecrating them as my priests. Procure a young bull and two unblemished rams. ²With fine wheat flour make unleavened cakes mixed with oil, and unleavened wafers spread with oil, ³and put them in a basket. Take the basket of them along with the bullock and the two rams. ⁴Aaron and his sons you shall also bring to the entrance of the meeting tent, and there wash them with water. ⁵Take the vestments and clothe Aaron with the tunic, the robe of the ephod, the ephod itself, and the breastpiece, fastening the embroidered belt of the ephod around him. ⁶Put the miter on his head, the sacred diadem on the miter. ⁷Then take the anointing oil and anoint him with it, pouring it on his head. ⁸Bring forward his sons also and clothe them with the tunics, ⁹gird them with the sashes, and tie the turbans on them. Thus shall the priesthood be theirs by perpetual law, and thus shall you ordain Aaron and his sons.

The text moves from a description of priestly vestments to the ritual of priestly ordination. It is assumed that Moses himself is to make the preparations and perform the rites for Aaron and his sons. "Consecrate" means to set apart for divine service. The ritual reflects elements that were added through the centuries down to the ritual performed by the Priestly tradition after the Exile.

The first stage of the ritual is done in several parts. First, all the sacrificial animals and the cereal offerings are to be brought to the entrance of the tent along with Aaron and his sons. Second, those to be ordained are ritually washed as a sign of purification, probably at the laver described in 30:17f. Third, they are ceremonially vested with the garments symbolizing their office. Fourth, the anointing oil (30:22f.) is poured over the heads of those being ordained.

29:10-45 Ordination Sacrifices

¹⁰"Now bring forward the bullock in front of the meeting tent. There Aaron and his sons shall lay their hands on its head. ¹¹Then slaughter the bullock before the LORD, at the entrance of the meeting tent. ¹²Take some of its blood and with your finger put it on the horns of the altar. All the rest of the blood you shall pour out at the base of the altar. ¹³All the fat that covers its inner organs, as well as the lobe of its liver and its two kidneys, together with

the fat that is on them, you shall take and burn on the altar. ¹⁴But the flesh and hide and offal of the bullock you must burn up outside the camp, since this is a sin offering.

¹⁵"Then take one of the rams, and after Aaron and his sons have laid their hands on its head, ¹⁶slaughter it. The blood you shall take and splash on all the sides of the altar. ¹⁷Cut the ram into pieces; its inner organs and shanks you shall first wash, and then put them with the pieces and with the head. ¹⁸The entire ram shall then be burned on the altar, since it is a holocaust, a sweet-smelling oblation to the LORD.

¹⁹"After this take the other ram, and when Aaron and his sons have laid their hands on its head, ²⁰slaughter it. Some of its blood you shall take and put on the tip of Aaron's right ear and on the tips of his sons' right ears and on the thumbs of their right hands and the great toes of their right feet. Splash the rest of the blood on all the sides of the altar. ²¹Then take some of the blood that is on the altar, together with some of the anointing oil, and sprinkle this on Aaron and his vestments, as well as on his sons and their vestments, that his sons and their vestments may be sacred.

²²"Now, from this ram you shall take its fat: its fatty tail, the fat that covers its inner organs, the lobe of its liver, its two kidneys with the fat that is on them, and its right thigh, since this is the ordination ram; ²³then, out of the basket of unleavened food that you have set before the LORD, you shall take one of the loaves of bread, one of the cakes made with oil, and one of the wafers. ²⁴All these things you shall put into the hands of Aaron and his sons, so that they may wave them as a wave offering before the LORD. ²⁵After you have received them back from their hands, you shall burn them on top of the holocaust on the altar as a sweet-smelling oblation to the LORD. ²⁶Finally, take the breast of Aaron's ordination ram and wave it as a wave offering before the LORD; this is to be your own portion.

²⁷"Thus shall you set aside the breast of whatever wave offering is waved, as well as the thigh of whatever raised offering is raised up, whether this be the ordination ram or anything else belonging to Aaron or to his sons. ²⁸Such things are due to Aaron and his sons from the Israelites by a perpetual ordinance as a contribution. From their peace offerings, too, the Israelites shall make a contribution, their contribution to the LORD.

²⁹"The sacred vestments of Aaron shall be passed down to his descendants, that in them they may be anointed and ordained. ³⁰The descendant who succeeds him as priest and who is to enter the meeting tent to minister in the sanctuary shall be clothed with them for seven days.

[31]"You shall take the flesh of the ordination ram and boil it in a holy place. [32]At the entrance of the meeting tent Aaron and his sons shall eat the flesh of the ram and the bread that is in the basket. [33]They themselves are to eat of these things by which atonement was made at their ordination and consecration; but no layman may eat of them, since they are sacred. [34]If some of the flesh of the ordination sacrifice or some of the bread remains over on the next day, this remnant must be burned up; it is not to be eaten, since it is sacred. [35]Carry out all these orders in regard to Aaron and his sons just as I have given them to you.

"Seven days you shall spend in ordaining them, [36]sacrificing a bullock each day as a sin offering, to make atonement. Thus also shall you purge the altar in making atonement for it; you shall anoint it in order to consecrate it. [37]Seven days you shall spend in making atonement for the altar and in consecrating it. Then the altar will be most sacred, and whatever touches it will become sacred.

[38]"Now, this is what you shall offer on the altar: two yearling lambs as the sacrifice established for each day; [39]one lamb in the morning and the other lamb at the evening twilight. [40]With the first lamb there shall be a tenth of an ephah of fine flour mixed with a fourth of a hin of oil of crushed olives and, as its libation, a fourth of a hin of wine. [41]The other lamb you shall offer at the evening twilight, with the same cereal offering and libation as in the morning. You shall offer this as a sweet-smelling oblation to the LORD. [42]Throughout your generations this established holocaust shall be offered before the LORD at the entrance of the meeting tent, where I will meet you and speak to you.

[43]"There, at the altar, I will meet the Israelites; hence, it will be made sacred by my glory. [44]Thus I will consecrate the meeting tent and the altar, just as I also consecrate Aaron and his sons to be my priests. [45]I will dwell in the midst of the Israelites and will be their God. [46]They shall know that I, the LORD, am their God who brought them out of the land of Egypt, so that I, the LORD, their God, might dwell among them.

The ordination is consummated by a series of three types of sacrificial offerings. Before each sacrifice Aaron and his sons were to place their hands on the head of the animal, symbolizing their identification with it. The young bull was to be offered as a sin offering. Its blood was to be placed on the horns of the altar to purify it and the rest to be poured out at the altar's base. The bull was to be completely burned, both on the altar and outside the camp, securing forgiveness of sins for those being ordained. The second sacrifice was the holocaust, the whole burnt offering. After the blood of the ram was splashed around the altar, its inner organs were washed and the whole animal burned on the altar.

The second ram sacrificed was the ram of ordination, a peace offering or communion sacrifice. Its blood was to be put on the extremities of the priests' right ears, hands, and feet, representing the purification of their entire body. Then the blood and anointing oil were to be sprinkled on the priests and their vestments, setting them apart for sacred ministry. Specified parts of the ram along with selected offerings of unleavened bread were to be placed in the hands of the priests and elevated from the altar and back to the altar ("waved") as a sign of dedication to God. Part of the sacrifice was burned on the altar, then the breast and thigh were given as food for the priests. They were to be boiled and then eaten with the remaining bread at the entrance to the tent.

The altar also is to be purified with the sin offerings and anointed. Its consecration will enable the altar to be used for special ceremonial sacrifices and sin offerings as well as the daily sacrifice to Yahweh. Every morning and every evening a lamb is to be sacrificed along with an offering of flour, oil, and wine. Thus, the opening and closing of every day was to be marked with offerings to Yahweh throughout every generation.

Verses 44-46 summarize the previous chapters concerning the Dwelling. God's meeting with the people of Israel makes holy the tent, the altar, and the priests. The God who continues to dwell among them is the very God who brought them out of Egypt. The purpose of Israel's institutions of worship is to enable Israel to continue to experience the life-giving presence of their liberating God.

30:1-10 Altar of Incense

[1]"For burning incense you shall make an altar of acacia wood, [2]with a square surface, a cubit long, a cubit wide, and two cubits high, with horns that spring directly from it. [3]Its grate on top, its walls on all four sides, and its horns you shall plate with pure gold. Put a gold molding around it. [4]Underneath the molding you shall put gold rings, two on one side and two on the opposite side, as holders for the poles used in carrying it. [5]Make the poles, too, of acacia

wood and plate them with gold. ⁶This altar you are to place in front of the veil that hangs before the ark of the commandments where I will meet you.

⁷"On it Aaron shall burn fragrant incense. Morning after morning, when he prepares the lamps, ⁸and again in the evening twilight, when he lights the lamps, he shall burn incense. Throughout your generations this shall be the established incense offering before the LORD. ⁹On this altar you shall not offer up any profane incense, or any holocaust or cereal offering; nor shall you pour out a libation upon it. ¹⁰Once a year Aaron shall perform the atonement right on its horns. Throughout your generations this atonement is to be made once a year with the blood of the atoning sin offering. This altar is most sacred to the LORD."

The instructions for the altar of incense are not given where we would expect, with the instructions for the ark, the table, and the lampstand. Like them, it is to be made of acacia wood and plated with gold. Like them it is to be placed in the holy place, but ready for movement with its golden carrying poles.

The altar is to be placed in front of the veil, apparently between the table and the lampstand. Incense was to be burned on the altar twice daily, near the time of the sacrifices. The incense was to be only the type prescribed in verse 34f. and no other types of offering are to be made on this altar. The altar is to be purified each year on the Day of Atonement by putting the blood of the sin offering on the horns of the altar.

30:11-16 Census Tax

¹¹The LORD also said to Moses, ¹²"When you take a census of the Israelites who are to be registered, each one, as he is enrolled, shall give the LORD a forfeit for his life, so that no plague may come upon them for being registered. ¹³Everyone who enters the registered group must pay a half-shekel, according to the standard of the sanctuary shekel, twenty gerahs to the shekel. This payment of a half-shekel is a contribution to the LORD. ¹⁴Everyone of twenty years or more who enters the registered group must give this contribution to the LORD. ¹⁵The rich need not give more, nor shall the poor give less, than a half-shekel in this contribution to the LORD to pay the forfeit for their lives. ¹⁶When you receive this forfeit money from the Israelites, you shall donate it to the service of the meeting tent, that there it may be the Israelites' reminder, before the LORD, of the forfeit paid for their lives."

Chapters 30–31 seem to be supplementary to the bulk of instructions that have preceded them. The directions contained in these chapters, though related thematically to the Dwelling, are not as closely joined as the previous chapters. The supplementary nature of these sections is indicated by the introductory phrase, "The LORD (also) said to Moses," (30:11, 17, 22, 34; 31:1, 12) which interrupts the lengthy sequence of divine instructions which precedes them. Their subject matter is miscellaneous and their sequence is somewhat arbitrary. However, they are all connected to Israel's worship and were judged to be important by those responsible for editing the traditions of Israel.

Why the taking of a census was considered dangerous is uncertain. Yet the practice is included here because it provided the financial support for Israel's sanctuary. Each one who registered, twenty years or older, was to pay a half-shekel as a "forfeit" or ransom to preserve him from harm. The instruction that everyone is to pay the same amount, rich and poor alike, indicates the equality with which all were to become "reminders" before Yahweh. It is probable that an earlier system of counting and taxation which provoked fear became in time a means of being united with the worship of Israel and remembered by Yahweh.

30:17-21 The Laver

¹⁷The LORD said to Moses, ¹⁸"For ablutions you shall make a bronze laver with a bronze base. Place it between the meeting tent and the altar, and put water in it. ¹⁹Aaron and his sons shall use it in washing their hands and feet. ²⁰When they are about to enter the meeting tent, they must wash with water, lest they die. Likewise when they approach the altar in their ministry, to offer an oblation to the LORD, ²¹they must wash their hands and feet, lest they die. This shall be a perpetual ordinance for him and his descendants throughout their generations."

The laver of bronze, used for ritual washing, was to be placed in the courtyard of the Dwelling between the tent and the altar of sacrifice. The priests were to cleanse their hands and feet before they entered the tent of meeting or before they offered sacrifice on the altar. The threat of death for not paying the half-shekel and for not washing emphasizes the close connection between Israel's worship of Yahweh and the gift of life given to each person by Yahweh.

30:22-33 The Anointing Oil

²²The Lord said to Moses, ²³"Take the finest spices: five hundred shekels of free-flowing myrrh; half that amount, that is, two hundred and fifty shekels, of fragrant cinnamon; two hundred and fifty shekels of fragrant cane; ²⁴five hundred shekels of cassia—all according to the standard of the sanctuary shekel; together with a hin of olive oil; ²⁵and blend them into sacred anointing oil, perfumed ointment expertly prepared. ²⁶With this sacred anointing oil you shall anoint the meeting tent and the ark of the commandments, ²⁷the table and all its appurtenances, the lampstand and its appurtenances, the altar of incense ²⁸and the altar of holocausts with all its appurtenances, and the laver with its base. ²⁹When you have consecrated them, they shall be most sacred; whatever touches them shall be sacred. ³⁰Aaron and his sons you shall also anoint and consecrate as my priests. ³¹To the Israelites you shall say: As sacred anointing oil this shall belong to me throughout your generations. ³²It may not be used in any ordinary anointing of the body, nor may you make any other oil of a like mixture. It is sacred, and shall be treated as sacred by you. ³³Whoever prepares a perfume like this, or whoever puts any of this on a layman, shall be cut off from his kinsmen."

The specially blended oil, made from aromatic ingredients and a gallon of olive oil, was to be used for the anointing of the tent and all the furnishings and implements of the tent and the court. It is also the anointing oil with which the priests were to be consecrated. Besides setting them apart for sacred functions, the oil also carried connotations of vitality and life. The anointed one was given vitality that was characteristic of the living God and received a share in the life of Yahweh. The various rituals of the Dwelling made use of blood, water, or oil—all symbols of participation in God's life.

30:34-38 The Incense

³⁴The Lord told Moses, "Take these aromatic substances: storax and onycha and galbanum, these and pure frankincense in equal parts; ³⁵and blend them into incense. This fragrant powder, expertly prepared, is to be salted and so kept pure and sacred. ³⁶Grind some of it into fine dust and put this before the commandments in the meeting tent where I will meet you. This incense shall be treated as most sacred by you. ³⁷You may not make incense of

a like mixture for yourselves; you must treat it as sacred to the LORD. ³⁸Whoever makes an incense like this for his own enjoyment of its fragrance, shall be cut off from his kinsmen."

Similarly unique and restricted to use in divine worship, the incense was to be burned on the golden altar of incense. Various spices and resins combined to provide a pleasing fragrance and a mysterious smokiness reminiscent of Yahweh's presence in fire and cloud.

31:1-11 Choice of Artisans

¹The LORD said to Moses, ²"See, I have chosen Bezalel, son of Uri, son of Hur, of the tribe of Judah, ³and I have filled him with a divine spirit of skill and understanding and knowledge in every craft: ⁴in the production of embroidery, in making things of gold, silver or bronze, ⁵in cutting and mounting precious stones, in carving wood, and in every other craft. ⁶As his assistant I have appointed Oholiab, son of Ahisamach, of the tribe of Dan. I have also endowed all the experts with the necessary skill to make all the things I have ordered you to make: ⁷the meeting tent, the ark of the commandments with the propitiatory on top of it, all the furnishings of the tent, ⁸the table with its appurtenances, the pure gold lampstand with all its appurtenances, the altar of incense, ⁹the altar of holocausts with all its appurtenances, the laver with its base, ¹⁰the service cloths, the sacred vestments for Aaron the priest, the vestments for his sons in their ministry, ¹¹the anointing oil, and the fragrant incense for the sanctuary. All these things they shall make just as I have commanded you."

Since God has specified that the materials for the creation of the Dwelling were to be the finest, it is appropriate that the artistry by which the Dwelling was created should also be the best. The choice of Bezalel as the managing artisan for the construction of God's Dwelling and of his assistant and other workers seems to be a logical conclusion to the long catalog of instructions which have preceded. It affords an opportunity to review all the furnishings, vestments, and supplies which they are to create.

There is a marked contrast between the dignity associated with work done in freedom and the brutal labor of slavery. God's spirit is recognized as the source of the artisan's skill, talent, and competence. There is pride and concern associated with mastery in the art of embroidery, metalwork, jewelry, and woodcarving.

31:12-18 Sabbath Laws

[12]The LORD said to Moses, [13]"You must also tell the Israelites: Take care to keep my sabbaths, for that is to be the token between you and me throughout the generations, to show that it is I, the LORD, who make you holy. [14]Therefore, you must keep the sabbath as something sacred. Whoever desecrates it shall be put to death. If anyone does work on that day, he must be rooted out of his people. [15]Six days there are for doing work, but the seventh day is the sabbath of complete rest, sacred to the LORD. Anyone who does work on the sabbath day shall be put to death. [16]So shall the Israelites observe the sabbath, keeping it throughout their generations as a perpetual covenant. [17]Between me and the Israelites it is to be an everlasting token; for in six days the LORD made the heavens and the earth, but on the seventh day he rested at his ease."

[18]When the LORD had finished speaking to Moses on Mount Sinai, he gave him the two tablets of the commandments, the stone tablets inscribed by God's own finger.

The instructions to observe the Sabbath serve as a conclusion to this section concerning the Dwelling. Having given directions for its construction and appointed workers for the task, Yahweh commands that all this work is to be done according to the six-day rhythm established by God's law. The Sabbath laws also conclude the establishment of the covenant on Sinai begun in chapter 19. The Sabbath is the sign of the covenant by which Israel was to be Yahweh's "special possession . . . a kingdom of priests, a holy nation" (19:5-6). By obeying the Sabbath the people of Israel would perpetually show that they are set apart, made "holy" by God (v. 13).

This observance of the Sabbath unites Israel with the rhythm of life as it was established by God. As God created the world in six days and rested on the seventh, so Israel was to create the Dwelling of Yahweh and continue to live in God's covenant marked by this weekly sign. The penalty of death associated with violation of the Sabbath again emphasizes the Sabbath's close relationship to life as Yahweh designed it. Disregard for the Sabbath is disregard for God who saved Israel from death and chose her to experience life in its fullness.

The two tablets of the commandments (31:18) contained the "ten words," a concrete summary of God's covenant with Israel. God's gift of the tablets fulfilled what had been promised as Moses ascended the mountain in 24:12. The inclusion formed by this promise and its fulfillment, into which the Priestly material concerning Israel's worship has been inserted, links the ethical law and the liturgical law of Israel. Likewise, the command to place the tablets in the ark of the covenant (25:16) binds the laws of Israel closely to their worship. The first obligation of this covenanted people was to worship their God.

32:1-29 The Golden Calf

[1]When the people became aware of Moses' delay in coming down from the mountain, they gathered around Aaron and said to him, "Come, make us a god who will be our leader; as for the man Moses who brought us out of the land of Egypt, we do not know what has happened to him." [2]Aaron replied, "Have your wives and sons and daughters take off the golden earrings they are wearing, and bring them to me." [3]So all the people took off their earrings and brought them to Aaron, [4]who accepted their offering and fashioning this gold with a graving tool, made a molten calf. Then they cried out, "This is your God, O Israel, who brought you out of the land of Egypt." [5]On seeing this, Aaron built an altar before the calf and proclaimed, "Tomorrow is a feast of the LORD." [6]Early the next day the people offered holocausts and brought peace offerings. Then they sat down to eat and drink, and rose up to revel.

[7]With that, the LORD said to Moses, "Go down at once to your people, whom you brought out of the land of Egypt, for they have become depraved. [8]They have soon turned aside from the way I pointed out to them, making for themselves a molten calf and worshiping it, sacrificing to it and crying out, 'This is your God, O Israel, who brought you out of the land of Egypt!' [9]I see how stiffnecked this people is," continued the LORD to Moses. [10]"Let me alone, then, that my wrath may blaze up against them to consume them. Then I will make of you a great nation."

[11]But Moses implored the LORD, his God, saying, "Why, O LORD, should your wrath blaze up against your own people, whom you brought out of the land of Egypt with such great power and with so strong a hand? [12]Why should the Egyptians say, 'With evil intent he brought them out, that he might kill them in the mountains and exterminate them from the face of the earth'? Let your blazing wrath die down; relent in punishing your people. [13]Remember your servants Abraham, Isaac and Israel, and how you swore to them by your own self, saying, 'I will make your descendants as numerous as the stars in the sky; and all this land that I promised, I will give your descendants as their perpetual heritage.'" [14]So the LORD relented in the punishment he had threatened to inflict on his people.

119

¹⁵Moses then turned and came down the mountain with the two tablets of the commandments in his hands, tablets that were written on both sides, front and back; ¹⁶tablets that were made by God, having inscriptions on them that were engraved by God himself. ¹⁷Now, when Joshua heard the noise of the people shouting, he said to Moses, "That sounds like a battle in the camp." ¹⁸But Moses answered, "It does not sound like cries of victory, nor does it sound like cries of defeat; the sounds that I hear are cries of revelry." ¹⁹As he drew near the camp, he saw the calf and the dancing. With that, Moses' wrath flared up, so that he threw the tablets down and broke them on the base of the mountain. ²⁰Taking the calf they had made, he fused it in the fire and then ground it down to powder, which he scattered on the water and made the Israelites drink.

²¹Moses asked Aaron, "What did this people ever do to you that you should lead them into so grave a sin?" Aaron replied, "Let not my lord be angry. ²²You know well enough how prone the people are to evil. ²³They said to me, 'Make us a god to be our leader; as for the man Moses who brought us out of the land of Egypt, we do not know what has happened to him.' ²⁴So I told them, 'Let anyone who has gold jewelry take it off.' They gave it to me, and I threw it into the fire, and this calf came out."

²⁵When Moses realized that, to the scornful joy of their foes, Aaron had let the people run wild, ²⁶he stood at the gate of the camp and cried, "Whoever is for the LORD, let him come to me!" All the Levites then rallied to him, ²⁷and he told them, "Thus says the LORD, the God of Israel: Put your sword on your hip, every one of you! Now go up and down the camp, from gate to gate, and slay your own kinsmen, your friends and neighbors!" ²⁸The Levites carried out the command of Moses, and that day there fell about three thousand of the people. ²⁹Then Moses said, "Today you have been dedicated to the LORD, for you were against your own sons and kinsmen, to bring a blessing upon yourselves this day."

After having spent many chapters of the narrative on the heights of Mount Sinai, the account sets up a dramatic contrast between God's will for Israel as revealed to Moses and the real world of human frailty. On the mountain is revealed the ideal covenant characterized by harmony with God's will in moral action and proper worship. In the valley below is displayed a serious act of disloyalty which threatens to destroy the covenant itself and plunge Israel into a situation far more deadly than their bondage in Egypt. The forty days on the mountain, shown by the account as a time of extraordinary revelation, was interpreted by the people below as an intolerable delay.

Chapters 32–34 stand between the narrative of God's instructions for the Dwelling and Israel's obedience to those instructions (chapters 35–40). The principal goal of the Exodus has been the freedom to worship Yahweh. That freedom now leads to disaster as the detailed instructions for constructing the Dwelling are followed by the hasty erection of Israel's idol. The elaborate preparations required to protect the holiness of God's presence in the Dwelling are contrasted with the impulsive and seemingly overnight construction of an impersonal object. Aaron's demand for the golden earrings to create the idol is a sharp digression from the instructions to collect gold and materials from the willing hearts of the people (25:2). Aaron and the people of Israel sought immediate access to their invisible and dynamic God through a passive, tangible image. The foundational principle for relationship with Yahweh, prohibition of the creation and worship of idols (20:4-5), had been violated.

Honoring the golden calf was not the worship of another god. It was an attempt to worship Yahweh by a means which Yahweh had already declared unacceptable. It was an attempt to represent God on Israel's terms—accessible, easily manipulated, passive and confined. The proclamation "This is your God, O Israel, who brought you out of the land of Egypt" mocks the absolute freedom of Yahweh who liberated Israel from bondage. The fact that they built an altar and celebrated a sacred feast with sacrifices to Yahweh indicates that their acts were outwardly religious but inwardly disloyal.

The form of the narrative has been influenced by countless instances of Israel's unfaithfulness throughout its history. The strongest influence is seen in King Jeroboam's later attempt to represent Yahweh with golden calves at the shrines in Bethel and Dan (1 Kgs 12:28). While the temple of Jerusalem claimed the ark as a visible assurance of God's presence, Jeroboam wanted to set up a substitute symbol in the sanctuaries of the northern kingdom. The narrative in Exodus is told in a way that makes it representative of all subsequent idolatry on the part of Israel. As the Dwelling is a paradigm of all Israel's worship, the golden calf is a paradigm of all Israel's unfaithfulness and sin.

The strong contrast between what happens on the mountain and what transpires in the valley is continued in the various reactions of God and Moses to Israel's sin. On the mountain, God's judgment is immediate and unambiguous. God intends to annihilate the covenant and begin a new nation with Moses himself. Moses, however, pleads for God to reconsider. In the valley below, Moses' anger flares against Israel, while God is convinced to relent.

Moses intercedes for Israel and seeks to persuade God to relent with three arguments. First, he argues that Yahweh has just liberated Israel from slavery and it would not be reasonable to reverse that action so soon. Second, he tells Yahweh that it would give the Egyptians great satisfaction to see Israel destroyed and it would endanger Yahweh's reputation among them. Third, he reminds Yahweh about the divine promise of land and progeny made to the patriarchs. The persuasive arguments of Moses lead to the awesome reversal of God's intentions. The account demonstrates much about Israel's understanding of Yahweh's nature. God's ability to be persuaded indicates that Yahweh is not a static, unchanging being; but rather the divine nature is personal, totally free, and responsive to the changing needs of a vital relationship with people.

Verse 15 begins the descent of Moses to the people below and the suspense mounts as we wait for Moses' response. The uncompromising anger displayed by Moses when he saw the people's idolatry and revelry parallels the anger of Yahweh on the mountain. Moses proceeds with an unbroken series of violent actions in which he demolishes both the tablets and the calf. The tablets symbolize the covenant and the description that they were engraved by God on the front and back confirms that Yahweh is the source and authority behind them. Smashing the tablets indicates that from Moses' point of view, the covenant has been broken and terminated. The calf is utterly destroyed and made totally irretrievable as the people are made to ingest their own sin by drinking the ground remains.

Aaron seeks to dissipate Moses' anger by minimizing his own role and blaming it on the people. Aaron does not succeed with Moses as Moses had with God. Aaron accuses the people of being prone to evil while Moses had defended them before God's anger. Aaron divorces himself from responsibility by proclaiming that the calf came from the fire of its own accord while Moses took on the sin of the people to mediate their forgiveness.

Moses called Israel to make an uncompromising choice for or against Yahweh: "Whoever is for the Lord, let him come to me!" The Levites who came forward became the agents of Yahweh's judgment and displayed faithfulness even to the point of slaying their own kinsmen, family, and friends. They demonstrated the ability to provide Israel with religious leadership that would be loyal against all pressures to compromise the covenant. Israel's tradition assumed that such purging was required for the continuing life of the community. Such display of loyalty and zeal for true worship on the part of the Levites demonstrated that they should be the ministers of Israel's rituals.

32:30–33:6 The Atonement

³⁰On the next day Moses said to the people, "You have committed a grave sin. I will go up to the Lord, then; perhaps I may be able to make atonement for your sin." ³¹So Moses went back to the Lord and said, "Ah, this people has indeed committed a grave sin in making a god of gold for themselves! ³²If you would only forgive their sin! If you will not, then strike me out of the book that you have written." ³³The Lord answered, "Him only who has sinned against me will I strike out of my book. ³⁴Now, go and lead the people whither I have told you. My angel will go before you. When it is time for me to punish, I will punish them for their sin."

³⁵Thus the Lord smote the people for having had Aaron make the calf for them.

33 ¹The Lord told Moses, "You and the people whom you have brought up from the land of Egypt, are to go up from here to the land which I swore to Abraham, Isaac and Jacob I would give to their descendants. ²Driving out the Canaanites, Amorites, Hittites, Perizzites, Hivites and Jebusites, I will send an angel before you ³to the land flowing with milk and honey. But I myself will not go up in your company, because you are a stiff-necked people; otherwise I might exterminate you on the way." ⁴When the people heard this bad news, they went into mourning, and no one wore his ornaments.

⁵The Lord said to Moses, "Tell the Israelites: You are a stiff-necked people. Were I to go up in your company even for a moment, I would exterminate you. Take off your ornaments, therefore; I will then see what I am to do with you." ⁶So, from Mount Horeb onward, the Israelites laid aside their ornaments.

The sin of the people and its consequences are the focus of these verses. In Hebrew, "sin" occurs eight times in verses 30-34. The consequences of sin are inevitably harmful, and the future of Israel's relationship with God is put in serious jeopardy. Israel's sin creates a situation in which life and death hang in the balance.

123

Moses intercedes for the people in order to attain forgiveness of their sin, even offering his own life for the sake of the people's future. The "book" in which Yahweh has inscribed those chosen to experience freedom and life is an image taken from the ancient practice of registering citizens. Being struck from Yahweh's book expresses the natural consequences of sin which is falling from God's favor, back into slavery and death. Chapter 32 ends by showing Israel exposed to the inevitable repercussions of sin.

Chapter 33 introduces even worse consequences of Israel's sin. While Yahweh remains faithful to the promise of a future land and a messenger to guide them, God withdraws the divine intention to personally dwell in their midst. Since Israel built a golden calf instead of Yahweh's Dwelling, they have seriously threatened their relationship with God. God's intention to dwell with them (25:8; 29:45) has been negated.

Yahweh's decision, "I myself will not go up in your company," plunged the people of Israel into bitter grief. As a sign of their mourning, they took off their festive dress and any ornamentation. The people who were destined to be God's "special possession . . . a kingdom of priest, a holy nation" (19:5-6) are now called "a stiff-necked people" and threatened with extermination if Yahweh should dwell too closely with them.

While Israel's future looks bleak, God has not closed off any possibilities. The narrative is opened to the next stage of God's dealing with Israel by the divine statement, "I will then see what I am to do with you." Moses will continue to intercede; God will continue to respond. Yahweh is shown to be a God who is in genuine partnership with people, who remains open to the future. Israel realized that passively leaving the future in the hands of God alone is not what God desires. Through his intercession, Moses helps shape a future that is different and better than if he had remained silent.

Following the paradigmatic pattern of creation, fall, and renewal, Israel has moved from her creation as a people to her fall into sin. Expelled from God's personal and abiding presence, Israel's future is now uncertain. The passage is transitional; it prepares the way for what God will do next as God continues to sort out the possibilities with Moses.

33:7-23 Moses' Intimacy with God

⁷The tent, which was called the meeting tent, Moses used to pitch at some distance away, outside the camp. Anyone who wished to consult the Lᴏʀᴅ would go to this meeting tent outside the camp. ⁸Whenever Moses went out to the tent, the people would all rise and stand at the entrance of their own tents, watching Moses until he entered the tent. ⁹As Moses entered the tent, the column of cloud would come down and stand at its entrance while the Lᴏʀᴅ spoke with Moses. ¹⁰On seeing the column of cloud stand at the entrance of the tent, all the people would rise and worship at the entrance of their own tents. ¹¹The Lᴏʀᴅ used to speak to Moses face to face, as one man speaks to another. Moses would then return to the camp, but his young assistant, Joshua, son of Nun, would not move out of the tent.

¹²Moses said to the Lᴏʀᴅ, "You, indeed, are telling me to lead this people on; but you have not let me know whom you will send with me. Yet you have said, 'You are my intimate friend,' and also, 'You have found favor with me.' ¹³Now, if I have found favor with you, do let me know your ways so that, in knowing you, I may continue to find favor with you. Then, too, this nation is, after all, your own people." ¹⁴"I myself," the Lᴏʀᴅ answered, "will go along, to give you rest." ¹⁵Moses replied, "If you are not going yourself, do not make us go up from here. ¹⁶For how can it be known that we, your people and I, have found favor with you, except by your going with us? Then we, your people and I, will be singled out from every other people on the earth." ¹⁷The Lᴏʀᴅ said to Moses, "This request, too, which you have just made, I will carry out, because you have found favor with me and you are my intimate friend."

¹⁸Then Moses said, "Do let me see your glory!" ¹⁹He answered, "I will make all my beauty pass before you, and in your presence I will pronounce my name, 'Lᴏʀᴅ'; I who show favors to whom I will, I who grant mercy to whom I will. ²⁰But my face you cannot see, for no man sees me and still lives. ²¹Here," continued the Lᴏʀᴅ, "is a place near me where you shall station yourself on the rock. ²²When my glory passes I will set you in the hollow of the rock and will cover you with my hand until I have passed by. ²³Then I will remove my hand, so that you may see my back; but my face is not to be seen."

Though verses 7-11 are from a different tradition and clearly interrupt the narrative of Moses' intercession for sinful Israel, the passage has been edited into this position because it was such an important memory for Israel. The connection to the present narrative concerns the role of Moses as intercessor before God. The verses emphasize the intimate, "face to face" relationship between Moses and Yahweh. Because Moses is so close to God, there is some hope for Israel's future in their dialogue. All may not be lost for their future as Yahweh's people.

The passage also gives a retrospective view of how things used to be. Israel used to faithfully seek God's will in the meeting tent, worship God appropriately from their own tents, and look to Moses as their mediator with Yahweh. By showing that the people were once faithful, it gives hope that Israel might continue that devotion in the future despite their failure. The editors use the passage to suspend the action for a while as Israel's fate hangs in the balance.

The "meeting tent" described here is a much older tradition than the tabernacle described in the priestly tradition. It served as a place in which Yahweh would periodically meet with Moses and reveal the divine will. It was at some distance outside the camp, whereas the tabernacle was to be placed in the midst of the people (25:8). The meeting tent was attended by Joshua, not by a family of priests; it was a place of periodic encounter, not a permanent dwelling for Yahweh; it was a place exclusively for meeting with the divine, not a place for sacrifice and offerings. This earlier and simpler concept of Israel's meeting tent was later amalgamated with the priestly tradition and replaced by the more elaborate Dwelling.

Here again we find hints that the passage does not just record historical memory, but it also describes Israel's worship in every age either at the temple in Jerusalem or at other public shrines. The people would stand outside in prayer as the priest entered the sanctuary. When they saw the cloud of smoke rising from the incense altar, they would prostrate themselves in worship, knowing that Yahweh was truly present among them. The liturgical ritual described here assures the people of Israel in every generation that their worship of Yahweh is a participation in that foundational experience of relationship with God in the desert.

The narrative of Moses' intercession for sinful Israel is picked up again in verse 12 after the retrospective interlude of verses 7-11. Moses pleads with God to restore the divine presence with every argument he can think of, and God responds favorably to his requests. First, Moses reminds God that, although he has been told to lead the people on from there, God has not told him how this is to be done. Reminiscent of Moses' first question to God at the burning bush (3:11), Moses suggests that he cannot accomplish God's mission alone. Moses then presses his pleas on the strength of his intimacy with God and the favor God has found in him. Given this special intimacy, Moses suggests that he should be told God's ways, that is, what God's intentions are in this matter. Moses then reminds God that "this people" is indeed "your own people."

To Moses' masterfully convincing plea, Yahweh responds with assurance that the divine presence would be with Moses along the way. Yet, Moses continues his plea, almost as if he didn't hear God. The emotional intensity continues as Moses seeks to obtain from God further assurance, not only for himself, but for all the people of Israel. Moses reminds Yahweh that only the divine presence distinguishes Israel from all the peoples of the world. Finally, in verse 17, God concludes this brief but effective dialogue by affirming that Moses' arguments have been convincing and that the constant presence of Yahweh would be given to Israel as they leave Sinai.

Having won the assurance of God's presence, Moses asks for a personal experience of God's presence to demonstrate the reality of the divine promise. God grants Moses' request in a modified way. Since no one can look upon God and still live, God plans to grant Moses a revelation of the divine presence not in terms of a visible appearance but in terms of God's attributes. Yahweh will reveal to Moses not how God looks, but how God is. Yahweh will make the divine "goodness" (a better translation than "beauty") pass by and will pronounce the divine name. The theophany will not be a tangible manifestation of God but a revelation of God's essential nature expressed in a proclamation of God's name and a recitation of God's character.

This personal, mystical experience granted to Moses is described in anthropomorphic terms. God's own "hand" is used to prevent Moses from seeing the divine "face." When God has passed by, God will take away the hand so that Moses will be able to see the "back" of God. The back represents that aspect of God which Israel will continue to experience as God goes ahead of them and leads them on their journey. The imagery suggests that God's presence can only be partially and dimly grasped by human beings, even by one like Moses.

The personal name of God, as seen in 3:14, is an expression of the absolute freedom of God. It is further described here in verse 19 as expressing Yahweh's free choice to grant favors and mercy to whomever God wishes. Yahweh is a God who "passes by"; a God who is made known by divine actions, a dynamic presence described through images of motion. Yahweh is not like the other gods who could be captured or contained in some human dwelling, or that could be manifested in a visible image.

The passage expresses the unchanging nature of Israel's presentation of Yahweh in cultic worship. Surrounding cultures represented their gods through unveiling images in their ceremonies. Yahweh, however, was an invisible God who forbade Israel to represent the divine presence through images. The manifestation of Yahweh in Israel's worship was always through word. The revelation of God was expressed through a proclamation of the nature of God and all that Yahweh had done for Israel. God's people realized that the very name of Yahweh was in itself a promise of freedom and life.

34:1-9 Renewal of the Tablets

¹The Lord said to Moses, "Cut two stone tablets like the former, that I may write on them the commandments which were on the former tablets that you broke. ²Get ready for tomorrow morning, when you are to go up Mount Sinai and there present yourself to me on the top of the mountain. ³No one shall come up with you, and no one is even to be seen on any part of the mountain; even the flocks and the herds are not to go grazing toward this mountain." ⁴Moses then cut two stone tablets like the former, and early the next morning he went up Mount Sinai as the Lord had commanded him, taking along the two stone tablets.

⁵Having come down in a cloud, the Lord stood with him there and proclaimed his name, "Lord." ⁶Thus the Lord passed before him and cried out, "The Lord, the Lord, a merciful and gracious God, slow to anger and rich in kindness and fidelity, ⁷continuing his kindness for a thousand generations, and forgiving wickedness and crime and sin; yet not declaring the guilty guiltless, but punishing children and grandchildren to the third and fourth generation for their fathers' wickedness!" ⁸Moses at once bowed down to the ground in worship. ⁹Then he said, "If I find favor with you, O Lord, do come along in our company. This is indeed a stiff-necked people; yet pardon our wickedness and sins, and receive us as your own."

God's directive to cut new stone tablets like the first ones expresses God's willingness to begin again the relationship that has been broken by Israel's infidelity. Once again Moses is instructed to make Mount

Sinai a sanctified ground which no person or beast may approach except Moses (19:12). Again Yahweh will descend onto the mountain in a cloud and give a new revelation of the divine name and the divine nature.

At the burning bush Moses had asked God how he is to know if God is really with him. In response, God revealed the enigmatic divine name, Yahweh, "I will be who I will be." In response to Moses' renewed request for assurance of divine presence, God passes before him and again calls out the divine name, twice this time. Who Yahweh is has been demonstrated in the saving events of Israel's liberation from slavery, the deliverance at the sea, nourishment in the wilderness, and covenant on the mountain. Now, this same God of freedom and life speaks the divine name again, giving Moses assurance of God's personal presence in the continuing journey from the mountain and into the land of promise.

The description of the divine nature in verses 6-7 is part of an ancient profession of faith. It contains some of Israel's oldest understanding of who Yahweh is as it was expressed in liturgical ritual. The five phrases describing the nature of Yahweh express the implications of the divine name. Through her saving history, Israel had come to know Yahweh as merciful, kind, faithful, forgiving, and just. Before such a God, Moses could only prostrate himself in worship, acknowledge the sins of Israel, and implore Yahweh again for a sharing in the divine presence for all Israel.

34:10-26 Religious Laws

¹⁰"Here, then," said the LORD, "is the covenant I will make. Before the eyes of all your people I will work such marvels as have never been wrought in any nation anywhere on earth, so that this people among whom you live may see how awe-inspiring are the deeds which I, the LORD, will do at your side. ¹¹But you, on your part, must keep the commandments I am giving you today.

"I will drive out before you the Amorites, Canaanites, Hittites, Perizzites, Hivites, and Jebusites. ¹²Take care, therefore, not to make a covenant with these inhabitants of the land that you are to enter; else they will become a snare among you. ¹³Tear down their altars; smash their sacred pillars, and cut down their sacred poles. ¹⁴You shall not worship any other god, for the LORD is 'the Jealous One'; a jealous God is he. ¹⁵Do not make a covenant with the inhabitants of that land; else, when they render their wanton worship to their gods and sacrifice to them, one of them may invite you and you may partake of his sacrifice. ¹⁶Neither shall you take their daughters as wives for your sons; otherwise, when their daughters render their wanton worship to their gods, they will make your sons do the same.

¹⁷"You shall not make for yourselves molten gods.

¹⁸"You shall keep the feast of Unleavened Bread. For seven days at the prescribed time in the month of Abib you are to eat unleavened bread, as I commanded you; for in the month of Abib you came out of Egypt.

¹⁹"To me belongs every first-born male that opens the womb among all your livestock, whether in the herd or in the flock. ²⁰The firstling of an ass you shall redeem with one of the flock; if you do not redeem it, you must break its neck. The first-born among your sons you shall redeem.

"No one shall appear before me empty-handed.

²¹"For six days you may work, but on the seventh day you shall rest; on that day you must rest even during the seasons of plowing and harvesting.

²²"You shall keep the feast of Weeks with the first of the wheat harvest; likewise, the feast at the fruit harvest at the close of the year. ²³Three times a year all your men shall appear before the Lord, the Lord God of Israel. ²⁴Since I will drive out the nations before you to give you a large territory, there will be no one to covet your land when you go up three times a year to appear before the Lord, your God.

²⁵"You shall not offer me the blood of sacrifice with leavened bread, nor shall the sacrifice of the Passover feast be kept overnight for the next day.

²⁶"The choicest first fruits of your soil you shall bring to the house of the Lord, your God.

"You shall not boil a kid in its mother's milk."

Just as the foundational covenant had been based on Yahweh's wondrous deliverance of Israel from slavery into freedom, the renewed covenant is grounded in an experience just as marvelous. Yahweh had delivered Israel from the self-imposed bondage of deadly sin and, through divine forgiveness, brought her back to the freedom and life that God's presence provides. God promises to work awe-inspiring "marvels" among the people of Israel. On her part, Israel must maintain exclusive loyalty in her worship of Yahweh.

The marvels that God will work concern the events associated with Israel's inheritance of the Promised Land. God will drive out those occupying the land of Canaan when the Israelites enter the land. Israel must not enter into any covenant relationships with these peoples and must remove all the cultic objects associated with Canaanite worship. The sin with the golden calf remains the archetypal sin of Israel, representing the constant temptation to religious compromise and syncretism.

The laws enumerated here contain elements that parallel both the Decalogue (chapter 20) and the Book of the Covenant (chapters 21–23). The foundational commands are similar to those of the ten commandments: the prohibitions against having other gods and creating images of the divine (20:3-4). Here the expansions on the commands are related to the specific temptations that will face Israel in the new land. To the command to worship Yahweh alone is added the prohibition against alliances or intermarriage with other peoples. The ban on making images specifically forbids the casting of molten idols, a direct reaction to Israel's sin with the golden calf. As in the Book of the Covenant, we see how the implications are drawn from the general principles according to the challenges of particular historical circumstances.

The remaining laws present a broad summary of some of the most important obligations of the covenant. Emphasis is on those laws that set Israel apart from other peoples and those that deal with right worship. The laws previously given are still valid, though these newly stated laws need particular emphasis in view of the challenges that will face Israel in relationship to "the Jealous One."

34:27-35 Radiance of Moses' Face

27"Then the LORD said to Moses, "Write down these words, for in accordance with them I have made a covenant with you and with Israel." 28So Moses stayed there with the LORD for forty days and forty nights, without eating any food or drinking any water, and he wrote on the tablets the words of the covenant, the ten commandments.

29As Moses came down from Mount Sinai with the two tablets of the commandments in his hands, he did not know that the skin of his face had become radiant while he conversed with the LORD. 30When Aaron, then, and the other Israelites saw Moses and noticed how radiant the skin of his face had become, they were afraid to come near him. 31Only after Moses called to them did Aaron and all the rulers of the community come back to him. Moses then spoke to them. 32Later on, all the Israelites came up to him, and he enjoined on them all that the LORD had told him on Mount Sinai. ³³When he finished speaking with them, he put a veil over his face. ³⁴Whenever Moses entered the presence of the LORD to converse with him, he removed the veil until he came out again. On coming out, he would tell the Israelites all that had been commanded. ³⁵Then the Israelites would see that the skin of Moses' face was radiant; so he would again put the veil over his face until he went in to converse with the LORD.

"These words" which God commands Moses to write down refers to all the words Yahweh had spoken: promises, admonitions, and laws. Immediately after this command we are told that Moses remained on the mountain with God for a long period of time; "forty days and forty nights" generally refers to a period of extraordinary revelation. It is not clear from the phrase whether it was Moses or Yahweh who then wrote on the tablets the "words of the covenant, the ten commandments." However, the context implies that Yahweh wrote the ten commandments to replace the tablets that had been broken. The phrase forms an inclusion with 34:1 and concludes the promise that Yahweh had made at the beginning of the narrative. Thus, what Yahweh wrote, the unchanging principles of the covenant, is distinguished from what Moses wrote, the historically modified ordinances which apply the unchanging law to the challenges of particular times and settings.

The narrative of Israel's sin and renewal (chapters 32–34) concludes with Moses' descent from Mount Sinai. The emphasis is on reestablishing Moses' authority as Yahweh's representative in the eyes of the people, since that authority had been discredited through the people's sin. Moses' first descent had been met with rejection and rebellion (32:15f.); his present descent is met with reverence and awe.

Moses' radiant face after being in Yahweh's presence expresses the authority he receives from God. The verb translated here as "become radiant" has been the source of much confusion, since it is related to the Hebrew word meaning "horn." Thus older translations often misunderstood the text to imply that Moses had horns extending from his head (as in the art of Michelangelo and Chagall). A more literal translation would be "put out horn-like rays." The image suggests Moses having rays of light coming from his face. It is described as a shining which Moses was not aware of, a gift of God to Moses to reestablish his authority before the people.

Whenever Moses communicated with God, whether on Sinai, in the meeting tent or the Dwelling, and whenever Moses communicated

God's words to the people, his face radiated as an afterglow from the immediate presence of God. Once more God has provided Moses with a sign for the people, a sign that Moses could not provide for himself. The sign leaves no doubt about the divine source of the words Moses communicates to the people. Moses related to the people "all that the LORD had told him on Mount Sinai" and Moses would continue to relate all that God communicated with him. Only after speaking God's word did Moses place the veil over his face to indicate that he was no longer speaking in God's name.

35:1-3 Sabbath Regulations

> [1]Moses assembled the whole Israelite community and said to them, "This is what the LORD has commanded to be done. [2]On six days work may be done, but the seventh day shall be sacred to you as the sabbath of complete rest to the LORD. Anyone who does work on that day shall be put to death. [3]You shall not even light a fire in any of your dwellings on the sabbath day."

Chapters 35–40 detail how the commands given to Moses in chapters 25–31 were carried out. The two sections complement one another as instruction and obedience. It is obvious that much of the wording of the previous chapters is repeated here, often verbatim. This repetition is characteristic of the Priestly tradition and is intended to emphasize to Israel and its priests the importance of maintaining these symbols and liturgical practices as essential for its tradition.

This final section of Exodus demonstrates how God's promise to dwell with Israel is fulfilled. Despite Israel's sin, God's promises allow Israel to build the Dwelling in anticipation of God's coming to dwell among them. In light of the period of Exile in which the priestly tradition was edited, Israel is assured again that just as God went forward with plans for a sanctuary after Israel's sin in the past, so God would again dwell with Israel in a renewed temple.

This section begins where the earlier instructions on the mountain ended—with an emphasis on the Sabbath. This unique sign expressing Israel's God-given freedom and life forms a bridge, linking chapters 25–31 and chapters 35–40 together. The rhythm of work and leisure established for God's liberated people was especially important as Israel created its Dwelling for Yahweh.

35:4-9 Collection of Materials

⁴Moses told the whole Israelite community, "This is what the LORD has commanded: ⁵Take up among you a collection for the LORD. Everyone, as his heart prompts him, shall bring, as a contribution to the LORD, gold, silver and bronze; ⁶violet, purple and scarlet yarn; fine linen and goat hair; ⁷rams' skins dyed red, and tahash skins; acacia wood; ⁸oil for the light; spices for the anointing oil and for the fragrant incense; ⁹onyx stones and other gems for mounting on the ephod and on the breastpiece.

Moses' call for the collection is a review of materials listed earlier to be brought by the people for the construction of the Dwelling. Repeated emphasis is given to the fact that the offering is voluntary. Obedience to the commands of Yahweh is internally motivated, not just an external compliance.

35:10-19 Call for Artisans

¹⁰"Let every expert among you come and make all that the LORD has commanded: ¹¹the Dwelling, with its tent, its covering, its clasps, its boards, its bars, its columns and its pedestals; ¹²the ark, with its poles, the propitiatory, and the curtain veil; ¹³the table, with its poles and all its appurtenances, and the showbread; ¹⁴the lampstand, with its appurtenances, the lamps, and the oil for the light; ¹⁵the altar of incense, with its poles; the anointing oil, and the fragrant incense; the entrance curtain for the entrance of the Dwelling; ¹⁶the altar of holocausts, with its bronze grating, its poles, and all its appurtenances; the laver, with its base; ¹⁷the hangings of the court, with their columns and pedestals; the curtain for the entrance of the court; ¹⁸the tent pegs for the Dwelling and for the court, with their ropes; ¹⁹the service cloths for use in the sanctuary; the sacred vestments for Aaron, the priest, and the vestments worn by his sons in their ministry."

In addition to the call for material, there is a call for talent. The invitation to every skilled worker is not found in the previous instructions. Again, an inventory is given which serves as a preview of all that is to be crafted.

35:20-29 The Contribution

²⁰When the whole Israelite community left Moses' presence, ²¹everyone, as his heart suggested and his spirit prompted, brought a contribution to the Lord for the construction of the meeting tent, for all its services, and for the sacred vestments. ²²Both the men and the women, all as their hearts prompted them, brought brooches, earrings, rings, necklaces and various other gold articles. Everyone who could presented an offering of gold to the Lord. ²³Everyone who happened to have violet, purple or scarlet yarn, fine linen or goat hair, rams' skins dyed red or tahash skins, brought them. ²⁴Whoever could make a contribution of silver or bronze offered it to the Lord; and everyone who happened to have acacia wood for any part of the work, brought it. ²⁵All the women who were expert spinners brought hand-spun violet, purple and scarlet yarn and fine linen thread. ²⁶All the women who possessed the skill, spun goat hair. ²⁷The princes brought onyx stones and other gems for mounting on the ephod and on the breastpiece; ²⁸as well as spices, and oil for the light, anointing oil, and fragrant incense. ²⁹Every Israelite man and woman brought to the Lord such voluntary offerings as they thought best, for the various kinds of work which the Lord had commanded Moses to have done.

The free-will offering includes not only the giving of materials but also voluntary skilled work. For the first time particular mention is made of women, both for their contribution of personal jewelry and for their skilled spinning of cloth.

35:30-36:7 The Artisans

³⁰Moses said to the Israelites, "See, the Lord has chosen Bezalel, son of Uri, son of Hur, of the tribe of Judah, ³¹and has filled him with a divine spirit of skill and understanding and knowledge in every craft: ³²in the production of embroidery, in making things of gold, silver or bronze, ³³in cutting and mounting precious stones, in carving wood, and in every other craft. ³⁴He has also given both him and Oholiab, son of Ahisamach, of the tribe of Dan, the ability to teach others. ³⁵He has endowed them with skill to execute all types of work: engraving, embroidering, the making of variegated cloth of violet, purple and scarlet yarn and fine linen thread, weaving, and all other arts and crafts.

36 ¹"Bezalel, therefore, will set to work with Oholiab and with all the experts whom the Lord has endowed with skill and understanding in knowing how to execute all the work for the service of the sanctuary, just as the LORD has commanded."

²Moses then called Bezalel and Oholiab and all the other experts whom the LORD had endowed with skill, men whose hearts moved them to come and take part in the work. ³They received from Moses all the contributions which the Israelites had brought for establishing the service of the sanctuary. Still, morning after morning the people continued to bring their voluntary offerings to Moses. ⁴Thereupon the experts who were executing the various kinds of work for the sanctuary, all left the work they were doing, ⁵and told Moses, "The people are bringing much more than is needed to carry out the work which the LORD has commanded us to do." ⁶Moses, therefore, ordered a proclamation to be made throughout the camp: "Let neither man nor woman make any more contributions for the sanctuary." So the people stopped bringing their offerings; ⁷there was already enough at hand, in fact, more than enough, to complete the work to be done.

The overseers Bezalel and Oholiab have been given not only the skill to do all the work necessary for creating the sanctuary, but also the ability to teach those skills to others. All those whose hearts were moved to join in the work were given the ability to fulfill all the necessary tasks.

The response of the people in bringing their voluntary offerings was so exuberant that Moses had to decree that no further contributions were to be made. The text encourages future generations to respond as zealously to Israel's communal worship.

36:8-19 The Tent Cloth and Coverings

⁸The various experts who were executing the work, made the Dwelling with its ten sheets woven of fine linen twined, having cherubim embroidered on them with violet, purple and scarlet yarn. ⁹The length of each sheet was twenty-eight cubits, and the width four cubits; all the sheets were of the same size. ¹⁰Five of the sheets were sewed together, edge to edge; and the same for the other five. ¹¹Loops of violet yarn were made along the edge of the end sheet in the first set, and the same along the edge of the end sheet in the second set. ¹²Fifty loops were thus put on one inner sheet, and fifty loops on the inner sheet in the other set, with the loops directly opposite each other. ¹³Then fifty clasps of gold were made,

with which the sheets were joined so that the Dwelling formed one whole.

¹⁴Sheets of goat hair were also woven as a tent over the Dwelling. Eleven such sheets were made. ¹⁵The length of each sheet was thirty cubits and the width four cubits; all eleven sheets were of the same size. ¹⁶Five of these sheets were sewed edge to edge into one set; and the other six sheets into another set. ¹⁷Fifty loops were made along the edge of the end sheet in one set, and fifty loops along the edge of the corresponding sheet in the other set. ¹⁸Fifty bronze clasps were made with which the tent was joined so that it formed one whole. ¹⁹A covering for the tent was made of rams' skins dyed red, and above that, a covering of tahash skins.

36:20-34 The Boards

²⁰Boards of acacia wood were made as walls for the Dwelling. ²¹The length of each board was ten cubits, and the width one and a half cubits. ²²Each board had two arms, fastening them in line. In this way all the boards of the Dwelling were made. ²³They were set up as follows: twenty boards on the south side, ²⁴with forty silver pedestals under the twenty boards, so that there were two pedestals under each board, at its two arms; ²⁵twenty boards on the other side of the Dwelling, the north side, ²⁶with their forty silver pedestals, two under each board; ²⁷six boards at the rear of the Dwelling, to the west; ²⁸and two boards at the corners in the rear of the Dwelling. ²⁹These were double at the bottom, and likewise double at the top, to the first ring. That is how both boards in the corners were made. ³⁰Thus, there were in the rear eight boards, with their sixteen silver pedestals, two pedestals under each board. ³¹Bars of acacia wood were also made, five for the boards on one side of the Dwelling, ³²five for those on the other side, and five for those at the rear, to the west. ³³The center bar, at the middle of the boards, was made to reach across from end to end. ³⁴The boards were plated with gold, and gold rings were made on them as holders for the bars, which were also plated with gold.

36:35-38 The Veil

³⁵The veil was woven of violet, purple and scarlet yarn, and of fine linen twined, with cherubim embroidered on it. ³⁶Four gold-plated columns of acacia wood, with gold hooks, were made for it, and four silver pedestals were cast for them.

³⁷The curtain for the entrance of the tent was made of violet, purple and scarlet yarn, and of fine linen twined, woven in a variegated manner. ³⁸Its five columns, with their hooks as well as their capitals and bands, were plated with gold; their five pedestals were of bronze.

The order of construction follows a logical sequence, moving from the outer walls and frame of the Dwelling to its inner furnishings. These sections duplicate the earlier instructions with a few minor omissions.

37:1-9 The Ark

¹Bezalel made the ark of acacia wood, two and a half cubits long, one and a half cubits wide, and one and a half cubits high. ²The inside and outside were plated with gold, and a molding of gold was put around it. ³Four gold rings were cast and put on its four supports, two rings for one side and two for the opposite side. ⁴Poles of acacia wood were made and plated with gold; ⁵these were put through the rings on the sides of the ark, for carrying it.

⁶The propitiatory was made of pure gold, two and a half cubits long and one and a half cubits wide. ⁷Two cherubim of beaten gold were made for the two ends of the propitiatory, ⁸one cherub fastened at one end, the other at the other end, springing directly from the propitiatory at its two ends. ⁹The cherubim had their wings spread out above, covering the propitiatory with them. They were turned toward each other, but with their faces looking toward the propitiatory.

37:10-16 The Table

¹⁰The table was made of acacia wood, two cubits long, one cubit wide, and one and a half cubits high. ¹¹It was plated with pure gold, and a molding of gold was put around it. ¹²A frame a handbreadth high was also put around it, with a molding of gold around the frame. ¹³Four rings of gold were cast for it and fastened, one at each of the four corners. ¹⁴The rings were alongside the frame as holders for the poles to carry the table. ¹⁵These poles were made of acacia wood and plated with gold. ¹⁶The vessels that were set on the table, its plates and cups, as well as its pitchers and bowls for pouring libations, were of pure gold.

37:17-24 The Lampstand

[17]The lampstand was made of pure beaten gold—its shaft and branches as well as its cups and knobs and petals springing directly from it. [18]Six branches extended from its sides, three branches on one side and three on the other. [19]On one branch there were three cups, shaped like almond blossoms, each with its knob and petals; on the opposite branch there were three cups, shaped like almond blossoms, each with its knob and petals; and so for the six branches that extended from the lampstand. [20]On the shaft there were four cups, shaped like almond blossoms, with their knobs and petals, [21]including a knob below each of the three pairs of branches that extended from the lampstand. [22]The knobs and branches sprang so directly from it that the whole formed but a single piece of pure beaten gold. [23]Its seven lamps, as well as its trimming shears and trays, were made of pure gold. [24]A talent of pure gold was used for the lampstand and its various appurtenances.

37:25-29 The Altar of Incense

[25]The altar of incense was made of acacia wood, on a square, a cubit long, a cubit wide, and two cubits high, having horns that sprang directly from it. [26]Its grate on top, its walls on all four sides, and its horns were plated with pure gold; and a molding of gold was put around it. [27]Underneath the molding gold rings were placed, two on one side and two on the opposite side, as holders for the poles to carry it. [28]The poles, too, were made of acacia wood and plated with gold.

[29]The sacred anointing oil and the fragrant incense were prepared in their pure form by a perfumer.

The construction of the ark, table, lampstand, and altar of incense are described in sequence because they are all articles of worship for the holy place and the holy of holies. There is no new information added, though some details not related to the construction have been omitted.

38:1-8 The Altar of Holocausts

[1]The altar of holocausts was made of acacia wood, on a square, five cubits long and five cubits wide; its height was three cubits.

²At the four corners horns were made that sprang directly from the altar. The whole was plated with bronze. ³All the utensils of the altar, the pots, shovels, basins, forks and fire pans, were likewise made of bronze. ⁴A grating of bronze network was made for the altar and placed round it, on the ground, half as high as the altar itself. ⁵Four rings were cast for the four corners of the bronze grating, as holders for the poles, ⁶which were made of acacia wood and plated with bronze. ⁷The poles were put through the rings on the sides of the altar for carrying it. The altar was made in the form of a hollow box.

⁸The bronze laver, with its bronze base, was made from the mirrors of the women who served at the entrance of the meeting tent.

38:9-20 The Court

⁹The court was made as follows. On the south side of the court there were hangings, woven of fine linen twined, a hundred cubits long, ¹⁰with twenty columns and twenty pedestals of bronze, the hooks and bands of the columns being of silver. ¹¹On the north side there were similar hangings, one hundred cubits long, with twenty columns and twenty pedestals of bronze, the hooks and bands of the columns being of silver. ¹²On the west side there were hangings, fifty cubits long, with ten columns and ten pedestals, the hooks and bands of the columns being of silver. ¹³On the east side the court was fifty cubits long. ¹⁴Toward one side there were hangings to the extent of fifteen cubits, with three columns and three pedestals; ¹⁵toward the other side, beyond the entrance of the court, there were likewise hangings to the extent of fifteen cubits, with three columns and three pedestals. ¹⁶The hangings on all sides of the court were woven of fine linen twined. ¹⁷The pedestals of the columns were of bronze, while the hooks and bands of the columns were of silver; the capitals were silver-plated, and all the columns of the court were banded with silver.

¹⁸At the entrance of the court there was a variegated curtain, woven of violet, purple and scarlet yarn and of fine linen twined, twenty cubits long and five cubits wide, in keeping with the hangings of the court. ¹⁹There were four columns and four pedestals of bronze for it, while their hooks were of silver. ²⁰All the tent pegs for the Dwelling and for the court around it were of bronze.

Following the construction of the inner parts of the Dwelling, the construction of the altar of holocaust, the laver, and the courtyard in which they are to be placed is narrated. The new note concerns the construction of the laver from the bronze mirrors of "the women who served at the entrance of the meeting tent." The verb suggests some form of organized ministerial service performed by these women.

38:21-31 Amount of Metal Used

²¹The following is an account of the various amounts used on the Dwelling, the Dwelling of the commandments, drawn up at the command of Moses by the Levites under the direction of Ithamar, son of Aaron the priest. ²²However, it was Bezalel, son of Uri, son of Hur, of the tribe of Judah, who made all that the LORD commanded Moses, ²³and he was assisted by Oholiab, son of Ahisamach, of the tribe of Dan, who was an engraver, an embroiderer, and a weaver of variegated cloth of violet, purple and scarlet yarn and of fine linen.

²⁴All the gold used in the entire construction of the sanctuary, having previously been given as an offering, amounted to twenty-nine talents and seven hundred and thirty shekels, according to the standard of the sanctuary shekel. ²⁵The amount of the silver received from the community was one hundred talents and one thousand seven hundred and seventy-five shekels, according to the standard of the sanctuary shekel; ²⁶one bekah apiece, that is, a half-shekel apiece, according to the standard of the sanctuary shekel, was received from every man of twenty years or more who entered the registered group; the number of these was six hundred and three thousand five hundred and fifty men. ²⁷One hundred talents of silver were used for casting the pedestals of the sanctuary and the pedestals of the veil, one talent for each pedestal, or one hundred talents for the one hundred pedestals. ²⁸The remaining one thousand seven hundred and seventy-five shekels were used for making the hooks on the columns, for plating the capitals, and for banding them with silver. ²⁹The bronze, given as an offering, amounted to seventy talents and two thousand four hundred shekels. ³⁰With this were made the pedestals at the entrance of the meeting tent, the bronze altar with its bronze gratings and all the appurtenances of the altar, ³¹the pedestals around the court, the pedestals at the entrance of the court, and all the tent pegs for the Dwelling and for the court around it.

The amount of gold, silver, and bronze used in the construction of the sanctuary and its court, a summary of the voluntary offerings of the people, is itemized. Its listing serves to underscore again the unreserved generosity of the people and to testify to the magnificence of the place built for Yahweh's dwelling. The amount of these metals is indeed remarkable, though not at all unrealistic for Israel's later temple in Jerusalem. Such abundance was not at all unusual for divine and royal structures in the ancient Near East. The priestly tradition considered such opulence as entirely appropriate for the worship of Yahweh's presence among them.

39:1-21 The Vestments

¹With violet, purple and scarlet yarn were woven the service cloths for use in the sanctuary, as well as the sacred vestments for Aaron, as the LORD had commanded Moses.

²The ephod was woven of gold thread and of violet, purple and scarlet yarn and of fine linen twined. ³Gold was first hammered into gold leaf and then cut up into threads, which were woven with the violet, purple and scarlet yarn into an embroidered pattern on the fine linen. ⁴Shoulder straps were made for it and joined to its two upper ends. ⁵The embroidered belt on the ephod extended out from it, and like it, was made of gold thread, of violet, purple and scarlet yarn, and of fine linen twined, as the LORD had commanded Moses. ⁶The onyx stones were prepared and mounted in gold filigree work; they were engraved like seal engravings with the names of the sons of Israel. ⁷These stones were set on the shoulder straps of the ephod as memorial stones of the sons of Israel, just as the LORD had commanded Moses.

⁸The breastpiece was embroidered like the ephod, with gold thread and violet, purple and scarlet yarn on cloth of fine linen twined. ⁹It was square and folded double, a span high and a span wide in its folded form. ¹⁰Four rows of precious stones were mounted on it: in the first row a carnelian, a topaz and an emerald; ¹¹in the second row, a garnet, a sapphire and a beryl; ¹²in the third row a jacinth, an agate and an amethyst; ¹³in the fourth row a chrysolite, an onyx and a jasper. They were mounted in gold filigree work. ¹⁴These stones were twelve, to match the names of the sons of Israel, and each stone was engraved like a seal with the name of one of the twelve tribes.

¹⁵Chains of pure gold, twisted like cords, were made for the breastpiece, ¹⁶together with two gold filigree rosettes and two gold rings. The two rings were fastened to the two upper ends of the breastpiece. ¹⁷The two gold chains were then fastened to the two

rings at the ends of the breastpiece. [18]The other two ends of the two chains were fastened in front to the two filigree rosettes, which were attached to the shoulder straps of the ephod. [19]Two other gold rings were made and put on the two lower ends of the breastpiece, on the edge facing the ephod. [20]Two more gold rings were made and fastened to the bottom of the two shoulder straps next to where they joined the ephod in front, just above its embroidered belt. [21]Violet ribbons bound the rings of the breastpiece to the rings of the ephod, so that the breastpiece stayed right above the embroidered belt of the ephod and did not swing loose from it. All this was just as the Lord had commanded Moses.

39:22-31 The Other Vestments

[22]The robe of the ephod was woven entirely of violet yarn, [23]with an opening in its center like the opening of a shirt, with selvage around the opening to keep it from being torn. [24]At the hem of the robe pomegranates were made of violet, purple and scarlet yarn and of fine linen twined; [25]bells of pure gold were also made and put between the pomegranates all around the hem of the robe: [26]first a bell, then a pomegranate, and thus alternating all around the hem of the robe which was to be worn in performing the ministry—all this, just as the Lord had commanded Moses.

[27]For Aaron and his sons there were also woven tunics of fine linen; [28]the miter of fine linen; the ornate turbans of fine linen; drawers of linen [of fine linen twined]; [29]and sashes of variegated work made of fine linen twined and of violet, purple and scarlet yarn, as the Lord had commanded Moses. [30]The plate of the sacred diadem was made of pure gold and inscribed, as on a seal engraving: "Sacred to the Lord." [31]It was tied over the miter with a violet ribbon, as the Lord had commanded Moses.

The text continually emphasizes how the divine instructions given on the mountain were carried out in precise detail. Verses 1, 5, 7, 21, 26, 29, and 31 repeat the phrase, "as the Lord had commanded Moses." The text emphasizes the divine origin and authority of the cultic vestments as commanded through Moses, and the precision with which Yahweh's instructions are to be carried out.

39:32-43 Presentation of the Work to Moses

[32]Thus the entire work of the Dwelling of the meeting tent was completed. The Israelites did the work just as the Lord had com-

manded Moses. ³³They then brought to Moses the Dwelling, the tent with all its appurtenances, the clasps, the boards, the bars, the columns, the pedestals, ³⁴the covering of rams' skins dyed red, the covering of tahash skins, the curtain veil; ³⁵the ark of the commandments with its poles, the propitiatory, ³⁶the table with all its appurtenances and the showbread, ³⁷the pure gold lampstand with its lamps set up on it and with all its appurtenances, the oil for the light, ³⁸the golden altar, the anointing oil, the fragrant incense; the curtain for the entrance of the tent, ³⁹the altar of bronze with its bronze grating, its poles and all its appurtenances, the laver with its base, ⁴⁰the hangings of the court with their columns and pedestals, the curtain for the entrance of the court with its ropes and tent pegs, all the equipment for the service of the Dwelling of the meeting tent; ⁴¹the service cloths for use in the sanctuary, the sacred vestments for Aaron the priest, and the vestments to be worn by his sons in their ministry. ⁴²The Israelites had carried out all the work just as the LORD had commanded Moses. ⁴³So when Moses saw that all the work was done just as the LORD had commanded, he blessed them.

When all the work was completed, everything that had been made was brought to Moses. The expansive inventory, drawn from the separate narratives of construction, fittingly closes and summarizes the account of the construction. Only Moses, who had received Yahweh's instructions on Sinai, was able to determine whether everything that had been made was in keeping with the divine intentions. After inspecting all the workmanship and finding that it had been completed "just as the LORD had commanded," Moses blessed them. Now all is ready for the erection and furnishing of the Dwelling and the anticipation of Yahweh's indwelling presence.

40:1-33 Erection of the Dwelling

¹Then the LORD said to Moses, ²"On the first day of the first month you shall erect the Dwelling of the meeting tent. ³Put the ark of the commandments in it, and screen off the ark with the veil. ⁴Bring in the table and set it. Then bring in the lampstand and set up the lamps on it. ⁵Put the golden altar of incense in front of the ark of the commandments, and hang the curtain at the entrance of the Dwelling. ⁶Put the altar of holocausts in front of the entrance of the Dwelling of the meeting tent. ⁷Place the laver between the meet-

ing tent and the altar, and put water in it. ⁸Set up the court round about, and put the curtain at the entrance of the court.

⁹"Take the anointing oil and anoint the Dwelling and everything in it, consecrating it and all its furnishings, so that it will be sacred. ¹⁰Anoint the altar of holocausts and all its appurtenances, consecrating it, so that it will be most sacred. ¹¹Likewise, anoint the laver with its base, and thus consecrate it.

¹²"Then bring Aaron and his sons to the entrance of the meeting tent, and there wash them with water. ¹³Clothe Aaron with the sacred vestments and anoint him, thus consecrating him as my priest. ¹⁴Bring forward his sons also, and clothe them with the tunics. ¹⁵As you have anointed their father, anoint them also as my priests. Thus, by being anointed, they shall receive a perpetual priesthood throughout all future generations."

¹⁶Moses did exactly as the Lord had commanded him. ¹⁷On the first day of the first month of the second year the Dwelling was erected. ¹⁸It was Moses who erected the Dwelling. He placed its pedestals, set up its boards, put in its bars, and set up its columns. ¹⁹He spread the tent over the Dwelling and put the covering on top of the tent, as the Lord had commanded him. ²⁰He took the commandments and put them in the ark; he placed poles alongside the ark and set the propitiatory upon it. ²¹He brought the ark into the Dwelling and hung the curtain veil, thus screening off the ark of the commandments, as the Lord had commanded him. ²²He put the table in the meeting tent, on the north side of the Dwelling, outside the veil, ²³and arranged the bread on it before the Lord, as the Lord had commanded him. ²⁴He placed the lampstand in the meeting tent, opposite the table, on the south side of the Dwelling, ²⁵and he set up the lamps before the Lord, as the Lord had commanded him. ²⁶He placed the golden altar in the meeting tent, in front of the veil, ²⁷and on it he burned fragrant incense, as the Lord had commanded him. ²⁸He hung the curtain at the entrance of the Dwelling. ²⁹He put the altar of holocausts in front of the entrance of the Dwelling of the meeting tent, and offered holocausts and cereal offerings on it, as the Lord had commanded him. ³⁰He placed the laver between the meeting tent and the altar, and put water in it for washing. ³¹Moses and Aaron and his sons used to wash their hands and feet there, ³²for they washed themselves whenever they went into the meeting tent or approached the altar, as the Lord commanded Moses. ³³Finally, he set up the court around the Dwelling and the altar and hung the curtain at the entrance of the court. Thus Moses finished all the work.

This synopsis of the sacred place, the sacred objects, and the sacred actions is joined to a sacred time, the first new moon of the year after the Exodus from Egypt. The climactic summary follows the two-part structure of the Priestly account. Yahweh's instructions to Moses for setting up the Dwelling (vv. 1-15) parallel the commands of chapters 25-31; Moses' obedience to God's instructions (vv. 16-33) parallels the obedience of Israel in chapters 35-40.

The prominent verbs of verses 9-15 are "anoint" and "consecrate." The focus of this section is not only the construction of the Dwelling, but its dedication as the sacramental means of divine presence with Israel. The sanctuary and all its furnishings, as well as Aaron and his sons, are to be anointed. The oil filled them with a vitality that was a share in the life of Yahweh. It set them apart for sacred purposes, and gave them a share in the holiness of God.

Again the text emphasizes that the divine instructions were carried out by Moses without variation. The formulaic expression "as the Lord had commanded him" appears as a refrain after Moses fulfills each command (vv. 16, 19, 21, 23, 25, 27, 29, 32). Finally Moses finished all the work he had been given to do (v. 33).

40:34-38 God's Presence in the Dwelling

> [34]Then the cloud covered the meeting tent, and the glory of the Lord filled the Dwelling. [35]Moses could not enter the meeting tent, because the cloud settled down upon it and the glory of the Lord filled the Dwelling. [36]Whenever the cloud rose from the Dwelling, the Israelites would set out on their journey. [37]But if the cloud did not lift, they would not go forward; only when it lifted did they go forward. [38]In the daytime the cloud of the Lord was seen over the Dwelling; whereas at night, fire was seen in the cloud by the whole house of Israel in all the stages of their journey.

The goal of the priestly narrative of the Dwelling is reached—"that I may dwell in their midst" (25:8). When all was ready, God fulfilled the divine promise and came to dwell among the people of Israel. The conclusion of Exodus thus begins the corporate worship of Yahweh by the people of Israel.

The "glory of Yahweh," manifested on the mountain of Sinai in the descending cloud and fire, now fills the sanctuary. The presence of Yahweh, experienced by Moses in the faraway heights, now draws near and dwells with God's people. Moses could not immediately enter the sanctuary because God's glory filled it. As on Sinai, he awaited God's further invitation to approach and enter into the divine presence.

The conclusion of Exodus also anticipates Israel's ongoing journey through the wilderness and the entry into the land of God's promise. Yahweh is a God on the move, as unpredictable as the clouds, as unconstrained as fire. God's presence guides and protects the people of God as the journey continues.

Israel's foundational story, which had begun with the people's bondage to an unchanging system and to the oppressive presence of Pharaoh, now concludes with Israel in the service of the God who journeys with them, who cannot be held bound, who invites them to the ever-new challenges of freedom. God, who is the source and sustainer of all life, now dwells among the people to give them abundance of life on the journey to full life. As the story is retold in every generation, the people of God are called into covenant with the God of freedom and life. They are liberated and enlivened as the journey continues in every age.